MW00626061

Demo Day

Title: Demo Day: Three challenging houses taught me Words
Matter on my journey & yours

Copyright © 2021 by Melissa Walker
All rights reserved.

Published in the United States by Glory Story Publishing.

Unless otherwise indicated, scripture quotations are New
International Version.

All rights reserved. No part of this book may be reproduced or
used in any manner without written permission of the copyright
owner except for the use of quotations in a book review. For
more information, contact glorystorypublishing@yahoo.com.
Brief quotes are permitted with appropriate author credit.

Any resources (websites, books, etc.) are offered as a resource.
They are not intended in any way to be or imply an endorsement
by Glory Story Publishing, nor does Glory Story Publishing
vouch for the content of these resources for the life of this book.

Cover design by Sondra Howe and Melissa Walker
Cover illustrations by Beckett Walker
Edited by Lisa Luke Easterling
Interior design by Samantha Seidel

Printed in the United States of America
ISBN 978-1-7363624-0-2 (paperback)
ISBN 978-1-7363624-1-9 (ebook)

Demo Day

Three challenging houses taught me
Words Matter
on my journey & yours

Melissa Walker

Glory Story Publishing

Dedicated to my hubby, Craig, who walked this journey with me, even though it's full of struggles we would have never chosen.

Craig, I respect your perseverance, discernment, and faith. I love you with all my heart and am so thankful for you!

xoxoxo

Contents

TIMELINE

2007 - 2009	Lived in chinese drywall / sinkhole house
2009 - 2011	Lived in rental house while seeking answers for drywall repairs
2011 - 2017	Lived in house which we bought as a foreclosure
2017 - 2018	Lived in second rental house with mold toxicity and neighboring house with sinkhole
2018	Moved into modern farmhouse we built, small and a/c issues which led to carbon dioxide build-up

Introduction

Do you know the story of Charlotte's Web where a talented spider spins words into a web overnight? Templeton the rat finds the words in newspaper clippings during his scavenger searches. When the farmer believes the words spun into the web describing Wilbur the pig, everything changes. The life of this adorable pig, naturally cheered by the reader, is spared first by Fern's convincing words to her father, and then by Charlotte's words in the web. Words Matter!

My journey includes multiple houses that made me sick. Along my journey, I have learned that words matter much more than we realize. Words build up. Words can also tear down and wreak the havoc of a demolition day.

As I share my journey and what I have learned, I'll use this bold font to encourage you specifically with your

journey and struggles. This isn't just about my journey. You have one, too. Hopefully, reading my journey will bring you encouragement, perspective, and hope. What are you struggling with today?

I am married to an amazing man who is full of integrity, perseverance, and hard work. Craig and I built our first house, took the profit from it and moved into a gated neighborhood where we planned to raise our family. Three houses and much illness later, my heart hurts when I think of our oldest son at the age of five saying, "Mommy, I never knew our walls could make us sick." First was a house with toxic drywall and the unbelievable story that unfolded with it. Later, our second rental house with mold mostly affected me. Then, our well-built, sweat equity invested, beautiful modern farmhouse had carbon dioxide (CO_2) buildup. Life is a journey, and even though your journey likely has not included three houses with a toxic environment, it is my hope that you will find encouragement through the details.

My hope is that the passages in bolded italics will bring you encouragement along your journey. As these words jump off the page, let them settle into your thoughts. Far too often, we go through life without taking time to pause and find perspective.

1

LIFE TURNED UPSIDE DOWN

In January of 2006, we began building the home where we planned to raise our children. There was such excitement as we picked out our lot while the roads were still dirt in the new neighborhood. We walked step by step through the process of building with a builder. During the pregnancy and newborn phase of our second son, we watched the slab get poured, blocks go up, roof, framing, windows, walls and finishing touches put on. On April 27, 2007, it became our new home with our 3-year-old Braden and 9-month-old Blake. Sweet memories still fill our minds of our boys sitting on the new carpet on the open family room floor the first day as well as our first night "camp out" upstairs in the bonus room. I recall Craig and Braden laughing loudly as they got cold showers – we hadn't hooked up the gas service yet. Oops!

Over the next two years, we enjoyed projects and decorating. Adding warm paint colors to each room, backsplash in the kitchen, and other decorative details was fun. In 2008, we had an attractive kid-friendly pool, spa, and unique cave waterfall built to expand our living space. In 2009, we extended hardwood floors into the family room area and bought new furniture while having no idea we would only enjoy this home for three more weeks.

One evening in May, I sat in our new recliner in the corner of the house, which gave me a clear view of the family room, kitchen, and dining room while rocking our son. I vividly remember having a thankful heart and praying a prayer of thanksgiving, enveloped in a sense of relief at having our home fully decorated. Finally, we wouldn't have to dedicate any more time to the house.

It had become a home filled with memories... Cookie Monster & farm animal birthday parties, Christmas celebrations and Easter egg hunts, fun times in the swimming pool, boys playing cars down the hallway and puppet shows over the half-wall between the kitchen and hallway. The fun memories came to a halt on June 12th, 2009.

On that hot summer afternoon, our air conditioner

had stopped cooling *again*. After two years of frequent visits, we were on a first-name basis with our air conditioning service provider, Brian, who recommended that we have our drywall checked. He said the coils on the downstairs unit needed replacing for the second time, after having just replaced the coils in the upstairs unit for the third time only a week before. He reported to us that the coils had been black every time and his company had recently learned of a strong connection between that phenomenon and Chinese drywall outgassing. WOW! Our hearts sank.

A few months earlier when we had heard on the news reports of homes smelling like rotten eggs, I had said, "I can't even imagine that." *We were now those people with a toxic home.* It had never smelled like rotten eggs, but there was a construction smell that had never fully gone away, especially in the closets, stairwell, and bonus room where we had not added an extra layer of paint after moving into the house. As time had gone on, the sulfur and toxic gas had been affecting our home and our health. Our world abruptly changed as we put the pieces of the puzzle together.

As the day went on, our research began by contacting the EPA and Health Department and reading through multiple websites. We were shocked by the pictures we saw and reports we read. They were way too familiar!

We started to connect the dots. The mirror edges were turning black; we had just chalked it up to cheap builder-grade medicine cabinet mirrors — which they were — but we later learned this was not standard corrosion. Door stoppers and door hinges were black.

We had noticed these things and attributed them to poor/cheap craftsmanship. I had noticed the door hinges and had been meaning to clean the black away, but I thought maybe Craig had sprayed WD-40 on them. He had not, but I never took the time to ask him until that weekend. It also made sense why we had to purchase our third dishwasher the previous month, again attributing the first two to being bottom-of-the-line dishwashers that had received poor ratings. The first two dishwashers (both same models) being bottom of the line quality further explained why they could not withstand the toxic, corrosive environment.

From there we saw our house with a whole new set of eyes and noticed additional things…

Master bathroom: toilet valve and door stopper corroded.

Extra bathroom: shower bell corroded.

Electrical wiring: fire hazard, according to our electrician.

Refrigerator: copper piping to compressor corroded.

The physical effects on our home were only part of the nightmare. We were traveling often and we had just been away from the house for three days. Our oldest son had awakened very grumpy and we found ourselves once again frustrated that he had been so good while away but was so irritable once back at home. Later that weekend, I sat and wept when I read a report on-line that other parents had made this same observation about their children while living in their house that contained toxic drywall.

Again, we started to connect the dots. My mommy heart had been heavy that there was something affecting our family. Braden, 5 ½, seemed to be frequently fighting a cold. Historically a very healthy child, he had responded well to Airborne Jr. to boost his immune system. We would either shake the cold-like symptoms, or he would just get what seemed like a mild cold (stuffy nose, sneezing, cough, sore throat). When he had been what we considered truly sick, then his cold had lasted for a very long time. Since he'd had a severe egg allergy since birth, we retested his allergies but found no answers.

Before Chinese drywall entered our vocabulary, Blake, 2 ½, had rarely been sick. But the past month in the house, he'd had two runny noses lasting more than a week. Craig, who was also otherwise in good health, had been dizzy and lightheaded on several occasions while living in the house. One time in particular stood out when he was affected for two days, but it was usually first thing in the morning when he would wake up dizzy. He attributed it to stress or jet lag from traveling for work.

Looking back, we are thankful for the discernment and wisdom to detox naturally and boost our immune systems. Blake, being a baby when moving in there, has since struggled with food allergies and chemical sensitivity. I have, as well. Without giving more details than most would want to read, I will summarize by saying that we have been on a health journey to boost our immune system and eat as healthy as possible given our busy lifestyle.

Life felt like it had turned upside down. It all hit me and my Type-A planner personality hard as I stood in my closet packing boxes, not knowing where the next roof over our heads would be. We thought we would move back into our dream home one day, and that we just needed a rental house while we got it all figured out and fixed.

I tried to convince myself to keep the situation in perspective, that it was just a "house," but as my husband lovingly pointed out – it was our HOME! I knew it was just a house, yet there was still the desire for a home to have a place to retreat, rest, and make memories.

God was about to show me in tangible ways that He is the only one who can give me a peace which passes all understanding and provides retreat, rest and memories with my family.

This isn't said to sound religious, but shows where my heart has grown through an overload of circumstances.

2

THERE WAS OUR SIGN –
THE SIGN WAS GONE

Next up was finding an affordable rental house that wasn't old, dirty, or in foreclosure status but would allow our chocolate lab furry member and was available right away. Talk about a needle in a haystack! But it sure did become clear one day. I had gone to see one of those "no way" rentals and in my discouragement started driving through neighborhoods. On a corner lot, I saw a white plastic 'For rent by owner' sign with a phone number. I wrote the number down and left the guy a phone message. The next day, I drove Craig to the house, but the sign was gone. I just *knew* it was that house, but where was the sign?

As we talked to the owners, we learned that the terrible storm the Wednesday night prior had resulted in the 'For rent' sign blowing out of their yard. The sign never showed back up. We took this as our "sign." The house was owned by a friend of a friend and they moved out in a week. Some friends and my mom came through for us as they packed up about 2/3 of our home while we were getting the rental house situation settled.

That weekend between discovering the drywall and moving out, we knew that God gave us confirmation that even though we were surprised, He wasn't. One of the boys' devotion books we read together said, "What if God told your Mommy & Daddy to move? How would you feel?" Then, the next day at church, the sermon series was about Jonah in the whale. The pastor's comment "It's not about you" echoed in my head as I had just told Craig that same phrase the day before. I had told him that it may not be about us... it's about who we can help and how we can stand strong through God's strength and live that out for our sons and others around.

It is hard to stand strong when your Mommy heart hurts. Braden was crying at night because he was a preschooler struggling with this abrupt move. Blake was saying "no boxes – toys in my room – this house". It was heartbreaking.

Ten years later, I would love to tell

you that life is easy and has been full of sunshine, but it has not. I won't sugar-coat it: life has been hard and even those around us may not realize the struggle this has been for us. You, too have likely had struggles or are going through one now. Later, I will share how much more I have learned and the understanding that what I'm going through is not about me, because there's a much bigger picture.

Rental house waiting, boxes piled everywhere, and a looming question mark over our heads, we remained thankful for the great location and for being able to paint the walls with leftover paint from our house. While we slowly unpacked boxes, I was "spring cleaning" the entire time.

Mattresses and pillows were the first items to be replaced right away. However, we did not realize at first the full impact of the toxic sulfur gases on our belongings. Our boys would go to sleep feeling fine, and then a few hours later we would hear them in their rooms coughing. I asked Craig if we could move their furniture out to the garage for a few weeks, just to make sure that it wasn't what was bothering them each night. While we were moving the furniture out, we ourselves felt scratchy throats, and our arms were itchy from being against the wood furniture. We discovered that their soft wood furniture had soaked up the gases, too. So, a mattress on a metal bed frame and pajamas, underwear, and shorts/jeans in plastic boxes became our way of life. Stuffed animals were washed, but many didn't fare so well or dried smelling musty. The CDC said to air out items and they would be fine. The CDC did not live the journey of actually owning a Chinese drywall house, and I can tell you that things did not just air out. I tried! On a few beautiful sunny days, I aired out baby toys and Christmas decorations on the back porch. Not successful! It would have been nice to not have to get rid of Braden's first Christmas stocking. I can still see him as a newborn tucked inside that stocking for cute pictures. While I am not a materialist collector kind of person, I am very sentimental.

The rental house was to also be a season of frustration, tears, calls with the bank, calls with attorneys, and letters in the mail, alongside detoxing from the house, a miscarriage, and countless days of interruptions and endless bills. Still, we made the choice to continue to trust that God was in control and would work it all out.

Have you learned on your journey

this life lesson that we lived through, of choosing to be positive and expecting a good outcome? It's a continual choice – sometimes daily – and it means that we choose to trust that everything is going to work out, regardless of whether it's our preferred plan or not.

3

THEN CAME THE SINKHOLE

Early in 2010, we chose to put action to our words. Every day for a week, we went to our unlivable house and walked around it as a family while we prayed for God to bring a resolution. Neighbors were still scarce as the neighborhood was only partially built, but if they were looking out their windows, they would have seen us walking and talking aloud and our boys making a mark on the driveway. Seven marks on that last day, trusting in what we couldn't see and taking one step at a time – day by day.

Extremely high water bills began in December 2009 and the roof was leaking in a bedroom. An experienced roofer spent hours inspecting the roof and house and determined it was not a roof issue. Doors were not lining up, and cracks on the exterior wall began in March 2010.

Sinkhole 101 became our crash course as we learned more than we ever wanted to know about such things.

On top of the drywall legal documentation, we were then dealing with insurance, an attorney, inspections, and still more documentation for the sinkhole. However, we were so thankful for the timing: we were able to file an insurance claim, whereas if it had been a month later, our policy would not have covered it unless it had been catastrophic. I will be honest and say that at that point, we did pray that it would be catastrophic and that the whole thing would just go away so we could move on with life. Can't fault me for wanting a clear-cut insurance payout with no questions asked if our home-in-a-hole was deemed unlivable. But that was not God's plan!

The date May 15th was on my heart, but at first I didn't know why. Details unfolded as May 15, 2010 dawned a sweet day of friends and family members gathering with us at our Chinese drywall/sinkhole house to pray. In faith, we counted on God to bring resolution. Walking away from the bank was not an option for us either financially or with the high value we placed on integrity. We pressed forward day by day and continued to trust.

You may be reading this and thinking you can't relate to gathering with

a group of people to pray. In fact, you may even think that I'm some super religious person. Please let me assure you that I'm no Bible scholar. In fact, it's not even about religion for me. It's about a relationship with my Creator who made our world, who made me and has proven faithful to meet all of my needs. Please keep reading, because this is about to resemble a movie script, down to the expert witness dying right before the trial.

Sinkhole reports showed sinkhole activity fifty-five feet deep and we decided to repair with helical piers and low-level grouting to stabilize the house. We were still planning to move back into the house and felt most comfortable with this repair instead of just adding the weight of grout without the reinforcement of the helical piers. Picture a house resting on strong stilts buried into the earth.

4

NOT NORMAL MEMORIES

What color are the lights you put on your Christmas tree? Early in our marriage, we compromised on classy white lights on the tree inside the house and the fun colored lights outside. However, while living in the rental house, I caved in. We had colored lights on the tree inside the house! It went against our tradition, but there was nothing normal about this timeframe in our lives, so colored lights it was.

Great memories were made in the rental house... Christmas with colored lights on the tree, Mickey Mouse & Monster Truck birthday parties, making a fort in the back bushes, building LEGOS at the dining room table as Braden entered that life stage as a little boy. Moving into a toddler bed and then a big boy bed were milestones with Blake.

Some memories we can look back on now and laugh about, though we didn't laugh then, like Craig losing his balance and almost falling inside the built-in wall unit while painting! Thankfully, I did not have to call 911 and say, "Help! My husband fell inside the faux wall of the entertainment set and can't get out!" He still teases me about my first response to him, which was, "Don't drip paint on the carpet!" In all fairness, I didn't realize from down below how badly he had slipped up high. Then there was that yucky snake on the back porch which struck at the shovel – the last thing it ever struck! Oh, and there's the time that I lit the outdoor grill and singed the wall. I haven't had to barbecue since then!

We saw God's faithfulness as He not only blew the 'for rent' sign out of the yard, but made Himself known in many other details, as well. God multiplied money when it didn't make sense so that we were able to pay the mound of bills from both houses. Most importantly, he gave us Beckett during this season of life in the rental house after a doctor had said we likely wouldn't have another child. This was the house where we brought Beckett home and where he lived the first five weeks of his life. January 20, 2011 was our rainbow in the middle of the storm when Beckett was born.

More changes were coming. The rental house was going into foreclosure and we knew that we needed to find a home before the bank set a moving date for us. We did not want a repeat of the last experience of packing while not knowing where we were going. My Type-A personality was stretched even further, as I certainly would never have planned to move with a five-week old baby! Timing seemed even worse as we were set to pack one particular weekend. Friends were busy with previous obligations. I sat home alone, tears filling my eyes as my heart was overwhelmed with exhaustion. Then, as a reminder that God is faithful, He had put it on a friend's heart to stop by after work and check on me. She packed so much that day! It was truly amazing.

Why do I share this? Because each of us has those times where we think we are at our wits' end and don't know how we are going to get it done or make it through. What are you facing along your journey where you are feeling overwhelmed, exhausted, alone? Hang in there, as there is sure to be help and hope even if it's at the very end of the day--or even this season in your life.

The house we were going to call home next had recently been posted as a foreclosure. But with paint, flooring, light fixtures, mirrors, and grass, we could make it our home. At this point, it was unlikely we would move back to our house after the drywall was repaired. Even so, the foreclosure price was a good investment and less than paying rent. This was confirmed as I was nearing the end of packing and tackling the stack of papers on the kitchen counter. Months prior, Craig had written on a notecard the addresses of a few houses. Among them was an address with the words "short sale" and an asking price of $50,000 more than we ended up paying. Timing. Not ours, but God's.

5

MOVING ON AND LEARNING SEMANTICS

With the sinkhole issue past, we were living in a house that belonged to us. In the background, the Chinese drywall issue lingered on. Walker vs. Teachers Insurance was our court case. We had found ourselves in a place we never thought we would be; we are not the kind of people who wanted any part of a lawsuit. It was an endless stream of documentation submissions to our attorney, inspections, conference calls and meetings in the judge's chambers. Our expert witness literally died mere weeks before the hearing (and we thought that only happened in the movies), then there were meetings in the judge's chamber at the courthouse in November and December of 2010.

Being very pregnant and knowing how this whole

situation had impacted our lives, it was not easy hearing the attorneys dispute semantics. The judge ruled in our favor on coverage in our policy, but with it being the only Chinese drywall case won against a homeowner's insurance company, it was a given that it would be appealed. The ruling was based on the definition of smoke. The comparison was if the hot water heater broke and flooded the house, then the hot water heater would not have been paid for, but the damages would be covered. So, all the damage caused by the off-gassing was covered, but not the cost of replacing the drywall. Semantics! Words matter!

The drywall house continued to occupy a large chunk of our lives. Negotiations with the HOA took away even more of our time. Over two years later, in February of 2013, we settled with our insurance company. The insurance check was nowhere near the cost of the bids we had received from contractors to repair the house. A month later, during a dinner date night, we decided to pull permits, contract the work, and pull out our own tools to join in.

After gathering more information, we had peace in April to proceed with construction and allow God to multiply the insurance check. On April 27th, we had our first family work day with our family of 5. We began by tackling the patio area. Picture a forest with weeds as tall as us — that was our patio. Twenty-five gallons of sludge was removed from the pool, and then we tackled the bushes (sorry, black snake, for disturbing your home). Before we left that night, I asked Craig if this was "Day 1" of the project and he said, "Yes, today is Day 1!" I shared with him that this was the sixth anniversary of the day we had purchased the house. Now this date had truly become DEMO DAY.

6

DEMO AND RESTORING TWO HOUSES

We were on a roll.

The second day of demo, May 1st, was an eventful one as our demo guy called to say he had ten workers in our front yard unable to work. A county inspector had just placed a red "stop work order" on the door, even though a permit was not needed for that part. My homeschool day with my boys came to a full halt. They tagged along as I was determined to problem-solve and keep us on schedule. A few hours later after a couple of phone calls, the "stop work order" was removed as it had been the inspector's error. A couple of hours later, the county called, saying the permit was ready. The county permit only took two days! That was a miracle. The next day, the house was demoed. Craig and I stood in the kitchen with insulation up to our knees and looked at each other with the question, "What in the world have we gotten into?" DEMO DAY had gone from exciting to "OH MY!"

The next day was a big day! May 7th, the company sprayed, foamed, and drenched the interior with a water-based biochemical disinfectant. Picture studs and concrete block, as that was all that was left after demo. This took care of any residue of the Chinese drywall. More excitement came on May 15th when our new drywall was delivered. May 15th was exactly three years after friends and family had gathered to pray with us. We learned along the way that numbers often have an association. The number 15 is associated with new. This new drywall was a welcomed sight.

Please know that these dates were not done by our doing — we only realized the connection of the dates afterward. I just have to believe that God enjoys giving us small details as reassurance.

That week was not without bumps in the road. The bank let us know that they were not going to be renewing the special Chinese drywall moratorium on our mortgage, so we were uncertain how that would unfold. We hoped the house would get sold sooner rather than later.

The drywall sat there while the insulation was installed. We shook our heads when an installer placed Chinese insulation between the studs. Thankfully Craig saw the randomly placed pieces of disgusting brown insulation which said "Knauff" on it. We knew that Knauff was a German company who sold a lot of "Made in China" drywall. We didn't even know that they made insulation, but we didn't want to even chance having anything in our house from that company! The insulation installers understood and kindly removed the brown insulation and replaced it with the traditional pink stuff.

In the midst of this busy week, we had numerous life-lesson conversations with our boys. I explained that while it was hard, we had to try to stay extra calm. We will meet a lot of people along the way and they are watching how we handle these tough situations. While Craig was talking with the insulation guy for the second time, the man said to make sure Craig told me that he had been praying for us. We knew this journey was about more than a house, and that the bigger picture is who we will meet along the way.

With countless projects, we were thankful for friends coming to help on June 1st, a big work day of finishing off outlets, installing ceiling fans, hanging doors, and landscaping.

Carpet was installed June 13th, so just for fun and because we could – we had a slumber party at the house. Sleeping on air mattresses with Beckett in the Pack-n-Play made for a fun memory. This marked four years since we'd learned about the toxic drywall and the first and only night Beckett ever stayed in that house.

June, July, and August were full of countless hours of projects. More doors, handles, ceiling fans, lights, toilets, sinks, faucets, shutters, closet shelves, mirrors, shower doors, towel bars, plants, mulch and grass, and a dishwasher installed, to name a few.

On August 5th, 2013, we sent this email update to friends...

It has been a while since we sent an update on the house. We have been doing numerous trips to Home Depot and Lowes and trying to finish the many details that come along with tearing a house apart and putting it back together. We are not weekend warriors anymore. The house is beautiful! Last week, we finished all of the inspections for the county and the bank. This week, we are contacting the bank to see what fees they may be willing to adjust and the plan is to put a for sale sign in the yard in the near future. It is an amazing, safe house for someone!

Every repair and restoration to this house was made the

best possible as if our family would move back there, because not only were we making sure it would be safe for anyone, we were not sure what the future held for us. But with the moratorium no longer an option, and the reality that financially it would be impossible to get caught back up with the bank, we put a FOR SALE sign in the yard in August. The Office of the President at our bank knew our case and had given us a moratorium where we had not paid the mortgage but were given time to find a resolution. Simply put, with all its issues, they hadn't wanted the house, either!

However, at this point, the Chinese drywall was gone and we were no longer eligible for the moratorium. Now, they were okay taking the house. Foreclosure was set to start on March 1st, 2014. During a Friday date night on Valentine's Day, we talked about how March 1st was only two weeks away. In a memorable conversation, we discussed our desire to be released from the time, energy, and money that the house had taken from us, but if it wasn't God's plan for a buyer, then we would count on Him to help our hearts through it. There was nothing else we could do. We fully surrendered.

Mid-morning on Monday, February 17th, our realtor called and said the wonderful words, "We have an offer." The next day we laughed when we learned that my cousin was the buyer's mortgage broker. For us, it was God's reminder that He is in the details. March 26th, 2014 was bittersweet for us. It's less than ideal to take money to closing when you are *selling* a house, yet we were thankful God had provided the money. We were able to show our boys integrity as we walked out having fulfilled the commitment we had made to the bank. It had been our prayer that if we couldn't move back into the house, it would bless a family who could and would enjoy it as much as we did – especially the great pool!

On the morning of the closing, we received an email from the buyers. Recently, I came across this printed copy of the email I had saved and it warmed my heart all over again as I read.

Craig, just wanted to take a moment to thank you and your wife for the card and well... a number of things. We spent the majority of the weekend moving stuff from storage into the house and although I am sore today, it was a huge relief knowing that we are reaching a resolution on all of this. You were extremely generous in letting us move items into the house prior to close and for that we are incredibly thankful. Already met a number of the neighbors and both my wife and I are excited about the neighborhood. I know of the issues that you had with the house but that it was also a place that you called your home. We both hope to fill it up with a lifetime of great memories. Here's to hoping for a smooth and painless close this afternoon! Regards, Jason

The closing was more than a closing on a house for us. At that time, I had written in my journal,

> "A book with many chapters – closing of the book on this house for us. Praise the Lord!"

Looking back, I see how that house was chapters in our book, but was by no means the full book. Randomly, we emailed updates to friends. Here's the last one we sent about this house....

Thank you for your prayers as we were on such a roller coaster of events leading up to the closing of the house and then a holding pattern. We know that the house situation brought us to full surrender as we gave the new owners the keys on Friday when the house did not close that day. We had tears on Thursday night as we left the house for the last time and prayed that our boys will remember God's faithfulness through this situation as well as how important it is to not do the easy thing in life but to do the right thing. (This was a sweet time as a family of five sitting on the half walls by the kitchen area.) We are happy to say that we closed on Monday night and the bank was sent the funds to pay off the mortgage yesterday. So, this is our official first day of being released from the house... it is starting to sink in that we are free from it.

On my computer, I had a document titled "Our Mess & God's Message", which held our timeline over the years.

To our boys –

Braden – you have been such a big helper and a hard worker through all of this house stuff. We are so proud of you and love you so much.

Blake – You are such a trooper and bring the fun (and mess) to projects. We know that God is healing and will continue to heal your body – love you bunches.

Beckett – You continue to amaze us and give us precious memories – just days ago you did some deep three-year-old thinking and asked, "Can we Facetime God?" Remember that even though you can't Facetime God on an electronic device, it is even better than that as we can seek His face through prayer and know He is always with us.

B1, B2 & B3 – Our prayer is that no matter what problems and trials you face in life, you will find peace and encouragement in knowing that God will take care of you. Remember that God's timing is not our timing. It's not easy, but it is okay. We love you with all our hearts and pray that you always love each other and God with all your heart!

Sitting at my computer six years later, those words are still SO AMAZINGLY TRUE!

No matter how many times I read through the last few pages, my eyes fill up with tears. Coincidence and happenstance are not part of life. Whatever your journey in life is holding for you, look beyond the circumstance and know that there's a big picture. But there are also many details that will most likely mean more to you later than they presently do. I encourage you to write down a brief timeline of your struggles; you will be glad you did one day in the future as you look back on the details and see the bigger picture.

While being released from the Chinese drywall/sinkhole house, we had been living in the house we bought as foreclosure, which we had made into a great home. Paint and grass make an amazing difference! It was a one-story with a bonus room upstairs, similar to our toxic drywall house. We loved our neighbors! There were constant texts about the kids going out to play--which almost always meant at least one parent going outside--as well as texts about who would like anything picked up from Costco or Trader Joe's.

On our one-third of an acre, we had a great area for mini kickball games in the front yard. The neighbors all knew the "bases": 1st base was a specific point in the flowerbed, 2nd base was the far tree, 3rd base was the tree beyond the sidewalk, and home plate was back to the "base" on the driveway. Our back yard had a pool with a beach entry and a fountain we thoroughly enjoyed! Yet, it was a costly house to maintain monthly, especially with the HOA fees (which covered only a gate that broke frequently). So, we decided to sell and build another house. Selling would mean getting a cash blessing at closing. Well water at the new build would mean no monthly water bill, a better insulated house would mean a lower electric bill, no HOA, etc. It all added up.

We have always tried to live as debt-free as possible other than a mortgage and a zero-percent-interest car payment. In 2015, Craig's company downsized from 49 people to 13 people and he welcomed the opportunity to not travel all over the country with no week's schedule ever being the same. With a new employer and less pay, we knew that we should take steps to diminish the house bills.

In 2016, two side-by-side one-acre lots went on the market in a rural suburb area. An extra perk was that it was two lots down from friends! One of the two lots sold right away. We inquired about the other one, but as it was higher than our budgeted price, we waited.

Two months later, a sermon about not just being hearers but doers stepped on our toes about taking the steps needed to follow God's word in order to lower our monthly bills and live more debt-free. That week, we made an offer on that lot. The realtor informed us that there had been no activity on the property until two days prior and our offer was the third one. The next day, they accepted our offer. We closed on the property with thankfulness for God's confirmation.

7

BIG CHALLENGE

In June of 2017, we sold our home and moved into our second rental house. This was a chaotic search as we had encountered numerous closed doors. A variety of factors complicated our search as the rental market was hot and rentals got snatched up quickly. We toured several houses where we could visibly see and/or smell mold or some other weird odor. By this point in our journey, my son and I were very sensitive to smell, and even Craig smelled some odd scents that we knew to run from.

So, with two days until closing, we broadened our budget and search. Our need was a rental house with four bedrooms (so we could use one of them for storage instead of paying for a storage unit) and a fence for our yellow lab to enjoy. With our broadened search, we found a house in a very convenient location – and we would even be the first renters to enjoy the fresh paint and carpet. It felt clean, unlike most of the other rentals we had been inside.

There was one *big* challenge for me: the house directly behind us had an enormous crack in the front and stair-step cracks along the side. It screamed *sinkhole!* to me. Growing up in this same area, I had never heard of sinkholes. But with the change in the aquifers and water table, they have been occurring more over the past fifteen or so years. Well, Craig convinced me that my fear was not a reason to stop us since "houses don't just fall into holes" and we were down to no other options. This house was it. We got the keys, moved in, and closed on our house. What a whirlwind!

Less than two weeks later, we were out of town when a news feed came up that I watched over Craig's shoulder on his phone. Eight miles from our rental house, two houses were swallowed up by a sinkhole. In went their boat, RV, one house and then the second house within a very short timeframe. Thankfully, everyone involved was safe, but it was a horrific sight. Tears rolled down my face. Some people are afraid of spiders and snakes. I guess my fear is sinkholes.

The next month, from the lot behind us, I heard the too-familiar sound of banging made when the inspectors were working to determine if there was a sinkhole. Months passed before the sinkhole and the house were fully repaired. It was an opportunity to trust God and work through my fear.

So, with the desire to build and move on to where we were not backed up to a sinkhole house, we moved forward with construction. That is when we decided to share our story with others.

In February 2018, we began a blog titled landtohome. net, A family's journey to build a healthy home. Under the "Who are we?" tab, we wrote:

> We are a family of five with three boys ages 7, 11, and 14 and a yellow lab named Copper. In 2003 and 2007, we built our first two houses with standard home builders. Then, in 2009, we lived through the nightmare of realizing that our house had Chinese drywall and had not been safe for our family. It was a sulphur gas chamber! With limited funds, in 2012, we pulled permits and swam our way through the muddy waters of taking the house down to cinder block and stud and then rebuilding. From there, we have been led to this place in life, where we are acting as the general contractor (called owner-builder). Two reasons: (1.) It's very

important that we are able to choose products for our home which are healthier options, and (2.) It's a lot more cost effective.

Land to Home blog posts show pictures while building the house as well as the process of making it our home. We shared what we learned and how others can benefit by making their house a healthy home, too. One of my favorite blog posts was more personal and was posted in May 2018:

We have a well! How did we begin construction without a well? The answer: great neighbors and three hoses attached together!

The speed bump in the road of a delayed well was smooth sailing because of great soon-to-be neighbors. Are you a good neighbor? Have you ever been blessed by neighbors with whom you could enjoy a conversation when you went out to check your mail? Have you ever had a neighbor you could ask to borrow a cup of sugar for the cake you were in the process of baking? Have you ever borrowed red thread from a neighbor when your outfit came unsewn right before you were dashing out the door to a Christmas party? Have you ever had a two year old neighbor who excitedly shouts "hello" the moment your garage door goes up? Do you close your garage door before you even get out of your car and never see your neighbors? Are you a good neighbor?

Our life has been richer because of the people we have been able to call neighbors over the years. We miss our daily interactions with many of them. When we purchased this property, it met our requirements: kids to play with our boys, friendly neighbors to borrow a cup of sugar or another ingredient when you are struck with an "Oh no – I'm baking, but out of...." AND we have been blessed with neighbors helping us out before we even officially became neighbors. Our speed bump was not having a company who was available to install a well in a timely manner. Thank you, Brewers, for sharing your well water! We haven't been slowed down at all and are thankful that three hoses joined together allowed us to borrow water from our neighbor.

Do you need to get to know your neighbors? Don't get so busy that you don't take time to know the people who live around you! You will miss out!

Let's take a brief break to talk about neighbors. Do you know your neighbors? As hard as this journey has been to this point and continues to be, we know that if we had not been forced to move more times than we ever planned or desired, we would have missed out on meeting some great people we called neighbors and now call friends! If you go through your week and don't talk with your neighbors, then I challenge you to get to know them. Plan a dessert night in your driveway where everyone brings a sweet or salty snack. Open up your home and break the busyness of going into the house before the garage door closes. It might not be within your comfort zone, but you might be missing out on a great friend if you don't make an effort.

This quote from Gilbert Chesterton really hits home for me:
"We make our friends; we make our enemies; but God makes our next door neighbor."

Here's a quick, fun side story to make this point. I

was talking with a current neighbor who moved in two houses over from us. We have a lot in common with children the same age and both of us having a career in education. Through conversation, we learned that we graduated from the same high school a year apart, we lived in the same neighborhood, and both of our parents lived in that neighborhood until two years ago. Both of our parents moved from two-story homes to a single floor. They moved about fifteen minutes north to the same new neighborhood and now live only two streets apart. In a later conversation, we discovered that our childhood homes were even the same floor plan and even almost the same color when our parents sold them after living there for over 35 years. Our children now enjoy playing together along with other children who live along our street. Neighbors are meant to be.

8

BACK TO THE STORY

In October 2017, we found a hidden treasure. We really liked the large tree in the middle of the property until we learned that it was a cherry laurel tree. It was an invasive species with roots known to burrow into septic tanks, which made for an easy decision to take it down. With this decision came our first big cost vs. experience decision. Since cutting it down and hauling it away would have been over $1,200, we decided to cut it down ourselves and let someone else haul it away for less than half the original cost. Our oldest son was excited to learn how to use a chainsaw. I mean, what 14-year-old boy wouldn't be excited? *Gas power tools* – need I say more? Several hours later, the tree was down and hauled away.

HOWEVER, the best part for me is that on the

lower part of the trunk, the wood had grown twisted and was – no lie – heart-shaped. I was so thankful that as they cut it down, they had noticed this special part of the tree. When I saw it, I was overwhelmed with the peace that it was time to move forward with the permitting. What a detail! A heart-shaped tree trunk! God was in control and hid a heart in the middle of the property that we would call home.

The God-sized details kept me going through the difficult months ahead. During the nineteen months of living in the rental house, God was ever more evident and real to my family. Our faith was stretched by not only our house situation, but also by Craig's hernia surgery, Hurricane Irma, a drunk driver almost hitting our house, break-ins while we were out of town and the beginning of my health journey.

In September 2017, Hurricane Irma threatened to be a catastrophic storm. Not being homeowners at the time, we felt very ill-prepared as we scavenged for plywood. Craig covered the windows in the master bedroom and bathroom to be our safe room and we had a slumber party in there. This was not like any other hurricane we had encountered, as the storm literally lost form and turned into a category 1 as it went over us. It was a noisy night with lots of debris the next day, but the biggest challenge in our area was friends without electricity for the week. Our rental house did not have any issue and our power only flickered. Wow! I still look back at the way the eye of the storm dismantled, so thankful that the storm was calmed. Once again, we saw that God is in the details.

I am convinced that God cares for us and orchestrates those who cross our path. In October of 2017, my husband had inguinal hernia surgery. I could share details about God's timing with Craig finding a doctor who performed the surgical procedure he felt best for him with a natural approach of attaching the muscle together instead of mesh insert. God was in the details! The unexpected was how God was in the details for me, too. Three hours away from home, I was the anxious wife who had never sat in a waiting room while her husband had surgery.

First off, the surgery was scheduled weeks sooner than we had expected. The day prior, the doctor's office moved his appointment sooner in the morning. This Friday morning, I sat determined to trust God despite the emptiness I felt. Across from me sat a woman whose husband's surgery was just before my husband's. She was a sweet lady from Georgia whose husband was a chiropractor, and she spoke encouraging words about loving your kids. Hers were older and beginning to spread their wings, and they loved the Lord. It was God's timing. I don't remember her name, but I remember clearly that my thirty-minute conversation with her was God-orchestrated, and after she left, my emptiness was gone.

Happy St. Patrick's Day 2018! I woke up at three in the morning after hearing a crash. My first response was to look out the back windows at the sinkhole house behind us. It was still standing and no sign of anything wrong. Hours later when we left for church, we noticed the corner stop sign was in our yard and discovered that was likely the crash I had heard. After church, when we had time to actually examine the yard, we discovered what had happened. We were located on the corner lot, and a car had hit the sign (leaving grey paint marks on the post) and flattened the crossed metal street signs while plowing it into our yard. We saw tire tracks in the grass showing that the car had run over the stop sign and pushed it into the yard as the tracks came within less than five feet of the outer house wall and then curved back out of the yard and back into the street, leaving the sign behind along with a black plastic piece of the car. Just on the other side of that exterior wall was the bed where our oldest son lay sleeping.

The next afternoon, I was standing at the corner talking with a neighbor when I saw a grey car turning, its engine cover flapping underneath and hitting the road as it went by. When my husband got home, we went further down the long, curved road and saw the car with the loose cover and what looked like the indentation of a metal post in the front bumper. We knocked on the door not knowing what to expect, but we knew we must go out of our comfort zone to knock. A conversation with the young lady and her mom inside confirmed that the girl had been intoxicated and was unaware of what had caused the damage to her car. I am convinced there was an angel there protecting my son's bedroom wall and protecting the driver that night by turning her car back to the street.

This was a reminder to us that there are times when bad things – really bad things, sometimes – happen to us, and that there are also times when we are protected from those really bad things. The stop sign in the yard showed us His protection as we might not have noticed the tire marks in the side yard where we didn't usually walk.

Naturally, she was horrified that it happened without her knowing it, but she was also amazed at our calm reaction towards her. It is true that I was rather calm for a Mama Bear, but it's only because my heart was overflowing with thankfulness that my son was protected and safe.

Maybe you are reading this and thinking God has not been in the

details of your life. Please know that there are times when He is working and protecting us and we don't even know it. There are bad situations that happen and yet they could have been even worse. Does anything like that come to mind?

Please keep reading... our 3rd house situation might help someone you know who has a tightly built house and perhaps their air conditioner unit is oversized and/or they have a tight, energy-efficient house with a higher-than-normal level of carbon dioxide...

As if a hurricane, a hernia surgery, and a near-miss car accident was not enough while living in a house with a now-repaired sinkhole, there was a string of car robberies in the neighborhood and neighbors' houses hit by lightning. Since we were out of town, our driveway was packed full of cars and only the car of our dog-sitter was broken into. I say only and yet that was bad enough, but the good part is that he was able to get his stolen items back. That same week while we were out of town, two neighbors across the street in both directions had lightning strikes. One neighbor had it go in through their kitchen ceiling! I'm sure you can imagine that by this point, while we were thankful for the great location of our rental house and neighbors we had met, we were also ready to move to a calmer, quieter area.

It wasn't long before the reality hit that this house had impacted me more than I was realizing. Exhaustion. Headaches. Restless sleep. Waking up with my heart racing. Sensitive to sounds. Extremely sensitive to smells. I knew something was off for me, but with the stress of life I continued to persevere through working as administrator for a unique private school that combines private school and homeschool, homeschooling my boys, building a house (I referred to that as our fun stress), keeping up with a recreational sports schedule for our boys, and being involved in church.

In October of 2018, I had my first (and hopefully last!) kidney stone. This resulted in an improper kidney infection diagnosis by a general physician who prescribed a high-dose antibiotic for three days. As it turned out, it wasn't an infection. Unfortunately, I couldn't turn back time. The antibiotic led to ice-pick pain up my neck with shrill headaches. After a few appointments with a functional medicine doctor, she helped me get to a better understanding of the root cause. I didn't like the results, yet it was nice to know that I wasn't imagining the exhaustion and other symptoms that were abnormal for me. Lab work led to the diagnosis of an autoimmune disorder, mold toxicity, and lead toxicity.

God is in the details. In November of 2018, I sat in a doctor's office for an IV to boost my immune system. This particular visit was on a Thursday morning. The only reason it was scheduled for that day was because I drove my son and some of his friends to a field trip destination seven minutes from my doctor's office so it made sense to leave for two hours for the IV instead of making the forty-five minute drive again on a different day that week.

Approximately half way through the IV, a woman from Colorado Springs sat next to me. She began to share with me about her mold toxicity and her autoimmune diagnosis which occurred during a very stressful year of her life. When she told me that I probably didn't want to hear her story, I encouraged her to continue talking. Oh, how I truly did!

She shared how she had homeschooled her four children. I was homeschooling my three boys. She was part of a group of families who helped start a Christian school in Houston. I started a Christian school. Later that evening, she texted me a few resources she had found helpful on her healing journey. A James 1 devotional was the last text. My new friend did not know that very morning I had read James 1 as I started my day and two hours later to the school staff. Out of the entire Bible... James 1! Not only do I think God has a sense of humor, but He is so faithful to orchestrate who we meet and give verses for us to cling to during good and not so good times.

Michelle and I had kept in touch. A few months later, she came back to town for more treatments and we met for dinner with our husbands. During that Friday night dinner, she surprised me with a sculpted eagle and a card with Isaiah 40:31. "Yet those who wait on the Lord will gain new strength; They will mount up with wings like eagles, They will run and not get tired, They will walk and not become weary." On Sunday, a box of curriculum was delivered and the enclosed note said "Thank you for your order...Isaiah 40:31." *I love it when God's details are so evident!* It's fun, encouraging and exciting. However, I am reminded that God is in the details in big and small ways--ways we don't always see and may never know. Again, our circumstances are not always about us!

If you are trying to do life on your own, I encourage you to consider how 2 Corinthians 1:3-4 (NLT) reminds us that it's not about us. It says "All praise to God, the Father of our Lord Jesus Christ. God is our

merciful Father and the source of all comfort. He comforts us in all our troubles so that we can comfort others. When they are troubled, we will be able to give them the same comfort God has given us." Do you know that empty feeling you have? The feeling that there's more than living and dying?

I encourage you (maybe even challenge you) to ask God to make you more aware of the details in your life. We have a friend who often asks people he meets, "On a scale of 1 to 100, how sure are you that you will go to heaven?" Think about that number and we'll come back to it later.

9

THE HOUSE WE BUILT TO BE OUR HEALTHY HOME

The very first night in our new home, I slept much better. I did not wake up with my heart racing in the middle of the night. Mold free sleeping! It was great to be in our home. The 1x1-inch heart in the wood of the front door made me smile. I was seeing a theme with hearts.

Looking back on the building process, it was good overall as we began in April and were "almost" completed in December. The "almost" part was the installation of the wood floors. Patiently (not by choice), we waited for the installation. The challenging part is that our flooring company was doing a demo and new install at a house located directly across the street from our rental house. In our large city. Out of all of the numerous houses. Really? This one, directly across the street where we were watching them come and work every day. Waiting our turn.

There were many head-scratching, head-turned sideways-in-confusion events during this first year in our house. One that stands out is our hurricane shutters. A friend of the family made the white metal accordion-style shutters that mount around each window and planned to have a co-worker drive them the three hours to our house and install them. The delay came when his warehouse caught on fire. The shutters were not only covered with debris, but trampled upon as the firemen gained access to the warehouse. Fortunately, their company was able to connect with another business to have the shutters remade, yet this necessitated us reapplying for a second temporary certificate of occupancy. Thankfully, it was not during hurricane season!

There were other memorable events, as well. One that kept me going and reminded me that words matter came in July. One highlight was the four Tuesday nights we hosted the middle-school boys from church. Pastor Andrew prayed the first night for the group to not just be hearers of the word but also doers. Almost three years prior, he had preached on that very topic the week we felt led to put in an offer on the very land where our home now sits. It is a simple trust, yet it's not always easy to act upon what we hear and know we should do.

So, at this point I fear that you might think I am making this up. I *promise* that's not the case! A reality show on TV wouldn't even know to make all of this up! This house became our 3rd house with challenges. For the record, it is now an amazing home and we are so thankful for the issues being resolved. It will be a great home for us until we know that it's time to sell it, and then it will be a super home for the next family who lives in it.

During the first year we lived in the home, we were walking through air conditioner issues with humidity building up in the house – especially the bonus room, where the unit was not cooling the space. While having the a/c company come to our house a dozen times, we did some research and discovered the problem. The company had told us they couldn't use the plans that had been drawn up by our draftsman's HVAC mechanical engineer, but would instead do their own. In hindsight, we see the huge mistake they made. But because they were the ones who had helped us discover the Chinese drywall, we had built a trust in this company and did not question them going with their own plans.

A year later as we sat in their office around a large board meeting-style table, we showed them the information and the expertise of the original mechanical engineer.

That day, Neil, the mechanical engineer, taught them how to fully operate their computer program, and that in fact our 5-ton downstairs unit should have been a 3.5-ton and the 1.5-ton upstairs unit should not have been more than a 1-ton. Bigger is not always better! Words matter *and* calculations matter! I will spare you the a/c education that we gained, but know that when a unit is oversized, it short-cycles and does not run long enough to move the air throughout the living space, which results in excess humidity.

Isn't that just like our lives? When our schedule is oversized, overloaded, or overwhelmed, we short-cycle – which looks a lot like a build-up of to-do lists, stress, and circumstances, all resulting in short-cycling ourselves and our loved ones. Are there areas of your life where you are short-cycling?

Monday, February 10th, 2020 felt like mountain-moving day! This was the day that we met with our a/c company and discussed our findings that the units were oversized. But after this meeting with the key people of the a/c company, we felt good about the outcome and resolution.

Once the air conditioning company understood

the problem and how it had happened, they attempted to make the situation correct by installing upgraded equipment in the form of variable-speed units, top-of-the-line wall thermostats, and dehumidifiers. Our hearts were full of thankfulness! Oh, how little we knew of the adventure still ahead! Throughout the journey, we consulted with various businesses and individuals. It was a sticky situation, as no one wants to come in and redo someone else's problematic set-up, and if they did, it would come with a hefty price tag. Since there's no money tree in our back yard, we persevered and sought answers while staying in constant communication with our a/c company.

While walking through our self-taught A/C 101, we learned about tight houses and the importance of air flow. I knew something was affecting my health, as I would wake up with a specific headache in the middle of the back of my head and felt unusually sleepy. Not tired or exhausted, but SLEEPY and eyelids heavy while trying to homeschool my boys. While researching, I learned that tight houses tend to have a build-up of carbon dioxide if the air is not ventilated correctly. My online purchase of a carbon dioxide (not to be confused with carbon monoxide) meter was bittersweet, as it was good to know that my symptoms were real and had a root cause, but not so good to know that our air conditioner system was still not operating appropriately - or safely.

We had discovered that the carbon dioxide was too high in our home and the system was still problematic. Through phone calls, we found a gentleman who lived four hours away from us who said he was too far away to help us directly but would consult as a pay-it-forward favor. We were so thankful! He helped us to confirm that the fresh air damper, dehumidifier, and a/c system were not interlocked. A turning point came with his suggestion to turn on the exhaust fans in the house to see if the carbon dioxide would lower. That improved the level of carbon dioxide, but leaving exhaust fans running was not a long-term answer; it was too noisy, not how it's supposed to be, and overall just not acceptable.

While walking through this frustrating, time-consuming situation, we remained on good terms with the air conditioning company. The running jokes were that they were coming to Thanksgiving dinner, as they were now like family, along with their opening of the garage door and saying, "Hi, I'm home!" We know they tried their best, but it just didn't get the job done.

This eventually led to our a/c company returning with a plan to correct the install. This turned into an additional 27 visits since they installed the correctly-sized units and dehumidifiers. There was a series of blunders with the installation, ductwork, and unforeseen issues, culminating in a very costly resolution. After over six months, we took on the huge expense of correcting the mistakes of the air conditioning company.

It was about this same time that we discovered that our on-going issue of the refrigerator's breaker flipping was not in fact a refrigerator issue, leaving us baffled as to why the service guys could never figure it out. We discovered that the installation of additional electrical outlets for the dehumidifiers over six months prior had placed them on the circuit dedicated to the refrigerator. Yikes! We are thankful that the breaker merely flipped and that there was not a worse outcome.

We grappled with frustration over the additional service visits to our home for the refrigerator, which had been not only inconvenient and needlessly costly, but had left us with the stressful practice of regularly checking on our refrigerator throughout the day to make sure it was on so that no food would spoil.

Isn't this just like life where we don't realize how one problem is affecting and complicating something else? Do you need to step back and look at your life's big picture and evaluate the details and the possible root cause of the bigger problem?

As I think about that key step of the equipment being interlocked, I think about another life lesson I have learned more recently. While reading definitions of the word "interlock," I read that it can be a verb or a noun. It is to lock together two or more things that fit together. Some synonyms are engage, interlink, and mesh. An antonym is disengage. With my health journey, I have learned the profound connection of physical, emotional, and spiritual health. Physical illness can show us changes needed in our bodies and lives.

I believe in healing. I am often encouraged by my friend, Trudy, who had stage-four lung cancer two years ago. She modeled for me the power of healthy eating and the importance of supporting the immune system to address deficiencies. She also modeled the practice of detoxing emotionally and allowing God to strengthen her faith. Our bodies were intricately designed so that all systems work together. If our physical, emotional, and spiritual lives are not in balance and meshed together, then our system does not function optimally.

> **What areas of your life are not interlocked? Have you ever thought of this connection before? What steps can you take to have better physical, emotional, or spiritual health? What are you allowing into**

your mind? Who can help you? These are questions I asked myself that proved to be very helpful, as sometimes we can get caught up in the fine print of life and miss the big picture. For me, it was remembering that I had to fight the tendency to get caught up in the details of daily circumstances, remembering the big picture that my life has purpose when I am loving others and living to glorify my Creator. It was also a time in my life which I realized that I had stuffed emotions, hurts, and disappointments deep down, so letting those go improved my physical and spiritual health. My a/c systems and my body systems are interlocked.

10

TOXIC THOUGHTS

Words build up. Words like *demo* and *tear down*. Sensitive to words – is this a real thing? Yes, it is. I became acutely attuned and sensitive to words – so much so that particular words and phrases felt like sandpaper on skin. I surveyed a group of friends and they responded with words and phrases that particularly irritate them. They shared some common utterings that I think we have all likely heard and possibly even said at some point. As I perused the survey results from friends, I noticed that phrases and words that spring from selfishness, those popped off as someone overreacts or shows judgement are not typically welcomed words. I would like to share a sampling of the toxic wordings shared with me.

With a heightened turmoil politically and socially, there are many words being overused, but some that come with particular negativity and judgement. These include: inequality, hypocrite, non-empathetic, unsympathetic, injustice, unfair, and identify, just to name a few.

The list of troublesome words, phrases, and thoughts continues...

* "Shorty"
* "I probably shouldn't say this, but..."
* "You didn't hear that from me, but..."
* Husband and wife bashing (It's never good, even if it's meant as a joke.)
* "I can't do that." (when it's more that someone is afraid or unwilling to try)
* "Are you done yet?"
* "Girl Power" (If you have to specify the power is for girls, then we must not actually have it.)
* "Boys will be boys."
* "We knew you are always so busy so we didn't invite you."
* "Get over it."
* "You don't know what you're talking about."
* "You're too...(much, sensitive, emotional, harsh, critical, intense, etc.)."
* "You should smile more."
* "You always look so perfect."
* "It was just a joke."

* "I know what you are going through." or "I know how you feel."

* "Can't you just relax?"

* "You make me feel guilty."

* "No offense, but..." (I've never heard this said without whatever follows actually being quite offensive, and unnecessarily so. Also, it's rarely said for anyone's edification except maybe the one who is saying it.)

* Any variation that uses God's name in vain, "Oh my god," "Gosh dang it," etc. (Look up https://www.gotquestions.org/OMG.html To me, it shows either lack of knowledge/ understanding of, OR complete irreverence for Him and His Word. If kids are around, I'm more likely to quickly say something like, "That's a precious name." in an effort to always speak from a place of love.)

* "What's your problem?" It is not a fun phrase to hear and there are far better ways to approach an issue that arises.

A friend who has been through numerous struggles while still shining with joy shared a phrase that really bothers her: "Do what makes you happy." She explained that when you live to be happy, you often become self-focused and tend to live for personal pleasure. God doesn't promise we will always feel happy

(1 John 16:33), but we can rest in His love, His plan, and His promise to bring good from everything He places on our path because He has overcome the world!

"Crazy" is a negative five-letter word. "That sounds crazy..." along with the looks, the pulling away that tends to accompany those phrases – statements involving this word tend to be sharply offensive. People generally don't want others to think they are crazy. The enemy loves to stir the pot of thoughts and words that rub us the wrong way, always looking to get the most mileage possible out of such abrasiveness.

A friend shared that after her experience in a house with mold, she grappled with the challenge of going through so much trauma and still feeling like she had to "prove it" (the trauma) to people to gain their compassion or support.

What's the word or phrase that hits you wrong and feels like sandpaper on skin or makes you cringe?

Negative thoughts and energy tend to manifest into physical issues, and that's when it gets our attention. If we allow it to go on too long, it can affect our mental state. Negative talk can not only be like the words and phrases above, but can be things like hearing someone complain, hearing gossip about someone else, or having someone go on and on about a subject such as politics without coming up for a breath of air. Negative talk markedly lowered my energy level.

Luke 6:45 says, *"A good man brings good things out of the good stored up in his heart, and an evil man brings evil things out of the evil stored up in his heart. For the mouth speaks what the heart is full of."*

This is a powerful quote to ponder: Karol K. Truman said, "Your feelings and thoughts create your attitudes and beliefs, which create your actions and behavior, which create your results and reality."

Sharing our stories opens the door for us to encourage others. Exhortation is a spiritual gift, so it comes more naturally for me to encourage others. But the reality is that we are to continually spur one another on and pray for each other. Sending a "thinking about you today" text can stop people in their tracks and help them feel loved when they are struggling through their day.

How good does it feel when someone compliments you? When I am tackling a ski slope or breezing through trees on a zipline and I receive a compliment or know that I am doing well, then my confidence is boosted and I enjoyed the adventure that much more.

You will become a negative and sick person if you think negative thoughts. Our hardships often start and stop in our mind. Usually, woe is me, selfish, here-and-now-perspective thoughts don't end well or lead to happiness and joy. Thoughts on what is really important in life, what is truth, and what is eternal present a powerful perspective.

You may have heard of the "bucket" example. As we have walked through my son's food allergies, we've discovered that sometimes a certain food may not trigger a reaction, and yet at other times he struggles to eat. Watery eyes, cough, and/or throat sensitivity have been common for him in the past. The way I explain it is that everyone has a certain sized bucket, and the more we put in, the more it will overflow.

What's in your bucket? My proverbial bucket was full of not just food allergies, but of life hurts and frustrations over house issues. When toxic thoughts would come my way, then my family knew that my bucket was spilling over. Buckets that spill over are messy and can flow out looking like a cranky mama. I venture to say that your bucket spilling over doesn't look so pretty, either.

Dark. Light.

Healthy. Diagnosis.

Frozen. Boiling.

Love. Hate.

Heaven. Hell.

Now. Eternity.

WORDS MATTER!

Let's look at the science...

Disease comes from dis-ease. An astonishing statistic is that 75 to 98 percent of mental, physical, and behavioral illness results from one's thoughts and emotions. Only a fraction of illness results from environment and genes. Recent research indicates that DNA changes shape as thoughts change! Anger, fear, and frustration result in DNA tightening and becoming shorter, which switches off DNA codes. However, here's the great news: gratitude, love, joy, and appreciation reversed and opened the DNA codes! Our mind is the catalyst behind what we say and do. Simply put, our thoughts drive our words and actions.

Scripture gives deep wisdom and encouragement:
"We destroy arguments and every lofty opinion
raised against the knowledge of God,
and take every thought captive to obey Christ."
2 Corinthians 10:5 (ESV)

"Cast all your anxiety on Him because He cares for you." 1 Peter 5:7

"Set your minds on things above, not on earthly things." Colossians 3:2

Your mind is in control over your body. You have likely heard this phrase and may have even said it yourself: "Mind over matter." While you cannot control your life circumstances, you can control your reaction to those situations. Finding peace amid crazy circumstances is a life lesson.

Stop and ask yourself: Are my thoughts life-giving or toxic? Are my thoughts leading to brain damage or brain function? Do my words speak life to myself and others?

Good thinking leads to good choices, which leads to healthy thoughts. Conversely, toxic thinking leads to bad choices which lead to unhealthy (toxic) thoughts.

Think about *The Little Engine That Could*. He thought he could, and then he did. It is a story of perseverance, but when you read it and realize that he kept telling himself he could until he did, then you see the power of his words. "I can't" or

"It's too hard" are negative thoughts that lead to a downward spiral instead of climbing the hill like the little engine. Negative thoughts lead to mental despair.

"Do not be anxious about anything, but in every situation, by prayer and petition, with thanksgiving, present your requests to God." Philippians 4:6

"Above all else, guard your heart, for everything you do flows from it." Proverbs 4:23

Words matter. Catch your thoughts, read and memorize scripture, and listen to praise music. The busyness of life can hinder our time to be quiet, take thoughts captive, and reflect. God-focused mindfulness pays off with a feeling at peace, gained wisdom, and likely healthier immune and cardiovascular systems. Remember, our bodies are an interlocked system.

Be intentional. Social media has crept stealthily into our lifestyles as a bombardment of information. Studies have added multitasking social media to the growing list of addictions. Social media overloads, over-compares, overruns family time, and overcomes self-control and feelings of self-worth. Shorter attention spans, lessening of emotional connectedness with others, and rising levels of stress have all been connected to social media use in the absence of intentionally-set and maintained boundaries.

We have daily choices. Relationships are a daily option. Social media is a daily option. Social media can act like an addictive drug in our brains. Much like a bombing of short bits of information, the stream of facts and opinions is a constant flow. The more social circles, the more stress. The more online multi-tasking, the more stress. Often, multitasking and stress lead to impulsive decisions and unhealthy eating choices. It's a daily choice.

> *"Finally, brothers and sisters, whatever is true, whatever is noble, whatever is right, whatever is pure, whatever is lovely, whatever is admirable – if anything is excellent or praiseworthy – think about such things."* Philippians 4:8

Stress. I have heard that stress is hard on your body. I have learned that stress is far more than hard; it wreaks havoc on your body. Get this: research indicates that stress is a factor in 75 to 85 percent of illness!

While we are sleeping, new baby nerve cells are created. Do your best to let them tear down toxic thoughts and build healthy thoughts. Lamentations 3:23 says, *"The Lord's mercies are new every morning. Great is Your faithfulness!"* Your brain can change and overcome. Research is showing that learning issues, depression, anxiety, OCD, and schizophrenia can be changed and do not have to become a way of life.

One of the most important factors in healing is a relationship with God. University of Miami researcher and professor Dr. Gail Ironson found that amongst HIV patients, the most significant factor in healing was when they chose not only to believe in, but to have a personal relationship with God.

What lies have crept into your thinking? Satan – the ultimate enemy of God's Truth – destroys with lies, unforgiveness, condemnation, doubt, and pride.

Take control. Clear the hurt off the landfill... It's "toxic trash thoughts" (say that ten times fast). Toxic trash does not disappear by putting on a happy face, showing up at a family event, pretending life is grand for the sake of the date on the calendar, or sticking our head in the sand like an ostrich. I think about my oldest son as a toddler, hiding his eyes in the couch cushion. He thought because he couldn't see us, he couldn't be seen. A "You can't see me – I can't see you" mentality does not work physically or emotionally.

Detoxing your thought life is the first step to changing your brain. In the same way that toxic thoughts can change your mental state, so can positive, happy thoughts.

You don't sit back and wait to feel better or put something off until you have a burst of energy. You have to choose happy and healthy. Your choices change your brain. It's called neuroplasticity.

Your brain is always thinking on a subconscious level, so you need to take control of what your brain is thinking on a conscious level. Your thinking is what changes your brain, which impacts the health of your body. Think about a positive future, pursue goals, and let faith, hope, peace, excitement, and health be the words at the forefront of your mind.

Where do you start? Start here. Commit to being intentional for 21 days. It takes 21 days to form a new habit and replace an old one. Research shows that it takes 21 days for protein changes in the brain. The science of protein changing is not something I will even attempt to summarize, but will simply say it is amazing! What's more, protein synthesis impacts genetic expression.

Confident in science and with a mindset of desiring thoughts of health and happiness for God's glory, let's make a decision to put mind over matter. As with all new things in life, we need to continue to practice and repeat healthy exercises. Continue to be intentional until you are automatically taking every thought and emotion captive.

"Let the peace of Christ rule in your hearts, since as members of one body you were called to peace. And be thankful." Colossians 3:15

"Now to him who is able to do immeasurably more than all we ask or imagine, according to his power that is at work within us, to him be glory in the church and in Christ Jesus throughout all generations, for ever and ever! Amen." Ephesians 3:20-21

If we could sit down to enjoy an iced tea, coffee, or smoothie, I would try to encourage you in this: it is very exciting news that our brains can change for the better. This science has advanced significantly, even in the past ten years.

Your core beliefs are a collection of your thoughts, feelings, experiences, and attitudes that impact how you interpret and experience life. Your subconscious core beliefs are like background noise. You do not want

your limiting core beliefs about a past trauma, fear, or illness to get in your way. What will you choose to be intentional about, knowing it could be life-altering on your journey?

11

WHAT WORDS DO YOU NEED TO DEMO OUT OF YOUR LIFE?

Let's look at two phrases: Have you lost weight? Have you gained weight? The change of one word makes someone want to pucker and kiss you or pull back and punch you. The change of one word is the difference between encouragement and discouragement. Words impact our perspective, our mood, our faith, our very life. Thoughts come from God, Satan, and ourselves. What do you and I choose to believe?

Let's look at a few words and how they matter. The educator in me thought about alphabetizing them, but for fear of it looking like a dictionary, I decided that was not a good idea. Then as I looked at the list of words, I discovered that there's actually a flow of how these words are connected, even though they may look random. This is NOT a dictionary of words! Let's dive into how they matter to both of us – you and me – in our respective journeys.

STUCK

There's a list of related words and synonyms: bamboozled, bewildered, breathless, confused, dumbfounded, floored, grid-locked, immovable, shipwrecked, static, stumped, submerged. Our society moves us at such a fast pace that it makes it easy to feel stuck, especially when we don't have a solid hope upon which to fix our eyes. Stuck can even be a feeling or response when the world is swirling around you in a state of busy.

Are you feeling stuck? Your challenges, struggles, unusual circumstances, or diagnosis DO NOT define you. Don't stay stuck.

ACHIEVEMENT/SUCCESS

Our world teaches a "keeping up with the Joneses" mentality. You know the unsaid expectations of the house with the picket fence, shiny cars, and children who look like they are ready to have a formal photo taken – ALL the time. None of these are bad things. It's when these things define our success that we gain a tainted perspective that will never bring us true contentment and satisfaction.

If your achievement and success were gone tomorrow, what would you have left?

HURTS

Conflict. Hurt. Accusations. Sin. As we walk through conflict, it is critically important to remember that other people don't always think the same way we do. Life perspective, lack of information, ignorance, bitterness, or sin they have experienced keeps them from seeing life the way you do. A pastor shared with me, "You can wrestle a pig, but the pig will just enjoy it." Our response can greatly determine where the hurt leads. Proverbs 15:1 instructs, "A gentle answer turns away wrath, but a harsh word stirs up anger."

What do we do? How do we respond?

FORGIVENESS

Forgiveness does not equal forgetting. It can feel like a huge battle to forgive as Satan uses resentment to lead to bitterness, which leads to unforgiveness and anger. Choosing to forgive is a choice. Forgiving does not mean going on a family vacation with someone who has deeply hurt you. Not putting yourself back in a hurtful situation is a healthy boundary that often needs to happen alongside forgiveness. You might be familiar with the Lord's Prayer in Matthew 6:9-13, but have you read the next two verses about forgiveness?

> *"Pray then like this: 'Our Father in heaven, hallowed be your name. Your kingdom come, your will be done, on earth as it is in heaven. Give us this day our daily bread, and forgive us our debts, as we also have forgiven our debtors. And lead us not into temptation, but deliver us from evil.' <u>For if you forgive others their trespasses, your heavenly Father will also forgive you, but if you do not forgive others their trespasses, neither will your Father forgive your trespasses.</u>'"*
> Matthew 6:9-15 (ESV)

WORRY/ANXIETY

Dr. Axe said, "It's not just your imagination; rates of anxiety really are increasing, especially among young people. Anxiety disorders are now the most common mental illness in the United States."

Alli Worthington stated in Breaking Busy, "Worry is different from anxiety. Anxiety is a deep sense of doom rooted in a fear that is often a lie from the Enemy. Anxiety cripples us and leaves us feeling incapable of escaping our situation. Worry, on the other hand, is our attempt to control the future."

79

"Do not be anxious about anything, but in everything by prayer and supplication with thanksgiving let your requests be made known to God."
Philippians 4:6

DOUBLE-MINDEDNESS

We can't feel one way, think another, and say something else while doing some other thing. We are to be congruent in our spirit, mind, words, and actions.

"For as (a person) thinks in his heart, so is he."
Proverbs 23:7 (NKJV)

TIMING

As I look back at all of the events, circumstances, and frustrations in my life, I know that it is all working out for me to tell you that even when we don't see it, God is working. While on a recent getaway to Blue Ridge, Georgia, our family of eleven people went tubing. All eleven of us were planning to go tubing on Tuesday morning until PopPop decided it was not going to be a part of his day after a very restless night's sleep. My sister-in-law said we didn't need to rush out the door quite as soon since we no longer had to be back to the house for his conference call. After a short drive down the road, we stopped at the first place to tube down the river, but with a two-hour wait, we decided to go further down the road to the next tubing place. As we arrived, the lady said we could fill out the form but not jump in the river at their location quite yet. They were watching a storm that was forming over the mountains. Quickly a storm rolled in, causing their power to go out. This was followed quickly by hail, lightning, and wind gusts that triggered the life jackets flying off the hanging posts like rapid-fire foam bullets from a toy gun.

After waiting out the storm under the partially covered areas, we learned about the severity of the storm. A large tree had fallen, blocking the road nearby and barely missing their van towing a trailer for the tubes. Rafters who had endured the storm on the river came back looking haggard and worn out! One of the moms reported that her seven- and nine-year-old children will likely never want to go tubing again. Another mom shared with us that her tube blew away in a gust of wind mid-river while they sought shelter along the side of the tree line.

Wow! Timing and details! If PopPop had slept great, we would have been out the door earlier and counted among those wind-whipped and beaten-from-the-storm people with the unfortunate experience of a hail and lightning storm on an open river. Timing matters. Details matter. Words matter.

PERSPECTIVE

I was reading a book with my son, titled *The Cow in the House*. It was a simple picture book, a story where a man's house was noisy because the bed creaked, the chair squeaked, and the roof leaked. As the story goes on, the man went to town to talk to a wise old man. Page by page, the story showed the man adding a noisy dog, cat, sheep, donkey and cow. The advice from the wise old man sounded silly, but he followed the directions by adding noisy animals one at a time. He yelled that the house was too noisy with a woof, woof, meow, meow, baa, baa, hee-haw, moo, moo, creak, squeak, and leak! The animals were sent outside. Inside the house, there only remained the bed creaking, the chair squeaking, and the roof leaking. The man thought the house was a quiet house. How his perspective had changed!

Are we sometimes like this? Life seems noisy with chatter, events, and circumstances that get added to our lives. Yet, when the noise is lessened, it makes it much easier to see the original noise of life. What are the noisy distractions in your life? When the "woof, meow, baa, hee-haw, moo, creak, squeak, and leak" stop, then what's your real perspective?

CREATOR

Sunsets. Mountains. Sandy beach with the waves crashing. The beauty of creation is evidence. Think about the Creator of the universe who made the mountains and knows every living creature in the depths of the ocean, yet He knows each of us. You may know about Him, but did you know that He wants to have a relationship with you? Jeremiah 1:5 says, "Before I formed you in the womb I knew you." Psalm 139:14 is one of my favorite verses as it reminds us that we are "fearfully and wonderfully made."

Do you believe in Him and have a relationship with Him? Is this something you are willing to think more about?

TRADITION

Tradition is one of those sneaky things that slips quietly into our decision-making. We find comfort in tradition. Routine can be found in traditions. We find happiness in looking forward to the Christmas Eve celebration followed by the morning of present-opening in our pajamas. My dad would always (as he still does when we go to their house to open gifts) be the one to collapse boxes and hold the large black garbage bag to stuff with torn wrapping paper. That is his thing. It works and it helps prevent the actual gifts from getting lost in a pile of trash and accidentally thrown away.

Some traditions like this are simple, and yet there are others that impact us more than we might stop to consider. Tradition can sneak in and shadow our decision-making regarding what is best for our season of life all 365 days of the year. Many various traditions surround Christmas, yet any of those can steal the focus from the actual reason that we celebrate the birthday of our Savior who came as a baby born in a manger.

Ally Worthington states, "Tradition is not a bad thing. But like any good thing, done with the wrong motivation (namely guilt and the pride of keeping up with the Joneses), traditions can shackle us to unrealistic expectations and a whole lot of unnecessary busywork."

SIN

This is a word we don't like to talk about. The "no, not me" comes out and we puff up our chest and put our shoulders back. The Hebrew definition of sin is "missing the mark" or "missing the point." You may have seen the acronym:

S   –   Self
I – Imposed
N – Nonsense

Definitions of sin can seem either vague or complicated, but it's actually a concept that even preschoolers can understand. Basically, anything we say, do, or think that is out of alignment with God, is sin.

I heard our child's pastor's wife KC Newbill share a great analogy about "just a little poop." She shared how one day her kids came in and asked if they could watch a movie. It was a questionable movie, with quite a bit of bad language and sexual content. Before answering about the movie she told them a story. "How about before we watch the movie, I make some brownies." They were excited at the thought. She explained that for the batter she would put water, oil, and eggs in the bowl, and before mixing it together she would go out back and get some dog poop from the yard.

"It's the same color as the brownies," she explained, assuring them they wouldn't really notice it. She asked for their input on how much poop she should gather. How much would be too much? They of course were grossed out and said they didn't want any poop in their brownies. As they reacted in disgust, she shared that it's the same with things we allow in through our eyes and ears. We are supposed to be very careful what we are allowing into our heads. Just as we don't want poop in our brownies, how many bad words are too many?

How many offensive scenes are too much? Tightening the filters in our lives and being very careful of what we let in allows us to live out Jesus' command to be Holy as He is Holy. That is the standard for our family.

> **Ask yourself: How much is too much? Think about that pan of brownies. A phrase you may have heard says, "Sin will take you farther than you want to go, keep you longer than you want to stay, and cost you more than you want to pay."**

EGO
Edging
God
Out

Sometimes fewer words are more. Think about this word as our human pride and sinful nature so easily get in our own way.

VULNERABILITY
What will people think? My grandmother wore heels, hose, dress, gloves, and a hat to church. It was her "Sunday best." She was a classy lady who dressed properly. As I've struggled to write the story we have lived through, I have thought about how our society

focuses on the outward and physical appearance. Unspoken rules of looking like you have life all together abound and continue to be a hindrance to being real and doing life together. For so long, people have tip-toed around anything that would not give a "Sunday best" impression. It's okay that we have imperfections. Give yourself permission to have flaws. Your vulnerability may help someone else.

Do you have the integrity to admit when you were wrong? Do you have courage to face your feelings and stuffed emotions to bring resolution?

INTEGRITY

Along our journey, integrity has been a value we have tried to model for our boys. As Pastor Phillip says, "More is caught than taught." One specific day, our youngest son caught and was taught a life lesson on integrity. That morning, we had cuddled on the couch while I read to him *Junior Discovers Integrity* by Dave Ramsey. The book defines integrity by explaining, "It's doing the RIGHT THING, even when no one is looking, and not expecting anything in return." At lunch time, we went to our local health and nutrition store, and just before we entered through the doors, there was a twenty dollar bill rolled in a rubber band. He picked it up and walked the money to a friendly face behind the counter. Ms. Darlene leaned down to the eye level of my eight year old son and complimented him on doing the right thing and how that showed integrity. As we walked away, he squeezed my hand and whispered his observation that she had used the word we had just read about. Yes, integrity. A few weeks later when no one had asked for their lost money, Ms. Darlene gave it back to him and we still keep it as a reminder.

Is there an area of your life where you are being challenged to do the right thing even when no one is watching?

OBEY

The Hebrew translation is "listen to" or "hear." In our culture, hearing doesn't mean action, but in the Hebrew, the word hearing equals following through. Hearing is obeying. As a parent, when your child hears your instruction but does not follow or take action, then they are not obeying. Obedience is often based on a relationship – a bond of trust, love, and respect. You may have heard the saying, "Delayed obedience is disobedience."

Is there something you are delaying but you know you should be doing?

Lastly…

GRATEFULNESS

One of my favorite words is "gratefulness." Our school theme last school year was "Make it a GREAT day!" I encouraged our teachers and parents with the importance of teaching our children that it's up to us to make it a GREAT day – for God, others, and ourselves. As an adult, I humbly admit that I haven't mastered this.

The following school year I expanded the "Make it a GREAT day!" to "Make it a GREAT-ful Day!" Of course, it seems ironic that a school is misspelling a word. We know it's spelled g-r-a-t-e-f-u-l, and we smilingly promised parents that students would end the school year knowing the correct spelling. Our hope was that most importantly, with our combined efforts, they would be impacted far beyond a spelling lesson by learning about gratefulness and how to live it out.

A few important things to know about this word:

* The opposite of discontentment is gratefulness. Do you see the importance of gratefulness?
*Being thankful does not come naturally. It must be cultivated. Gratefulness helps us to recognize that we have so much to be thankful for.
* Gratefulness gets our eyes off ourselves

and helps us to focus back on God. We must remember that life is ultimately about Him, not us.

*A heart of gratitude leaves no room for complaining. It's impossible to be thankful while filled with negativity.

Psalm 107:1 reminds us to "Give thanks to the Lord, for He is good! His faithful love endures forever."

Do you see why praise is so important? Praise helps us shut out the worldly desires that constantly pull on us and weigh us down. During a sermon, Pastor Kelly commented, "Worldliness begins where my gratitude ends." So, since we know that is true, then we can also say that gratitude begins where worldliness ends. 1 John 2:15-17 says not to love the world and the things of this world.

Gratefulness does not mean happiness or an easy life. Gratefulness helps us have the "abundant life" that God desires for us.

John Piper says, "Grumbling is an evidence of little faith in the gracious providence of God in all the affairs of our lives. And little faith is a dishonor to him. It belittles his sovereignty and wisdom and goodness."

What will you do in your home to cultivate gratitude?

One simple but impactful idea is a blessing jar, into which you place slips of paper with each family member's thoughts of thankfulness written down. Another idea is a gratitude journal where you write down what you are thankful for each day or as often as you wish to write. In *The Grumble Free Year*, Tricia Goyer explains how her family of 11- 2 parents, 8 kids, and a grandmother with dementia - strived to stop grumbling. She said, "Cultivating a grateful attitude is not for the fainthearted.

Lips that are quick to praise instead of grumble do not appear overnight." As she related their experiences, her encouraging words explained this further: "How can writing down gratitudes help? It is a physical way to celebrate a God-given emotion. Gratefulness is evidence of God working within our souls. Gratitude is an outpouring of what's inside, and taking note of our gratitude reminds our kids that when we are grateful, there's someone we need to thank: God."

12

WHAT'S YOUR NUMBER
FROM 1 TO 100?

Recalling the question asked earlier, on a scale of 1 to 100, if you were to die tonight, how sure are you that God would let you into Heaven? Think about any internal emptiness you may feel. New clothes, toys, or the latest technology may temporarily bring you happiness but can't fulfill the inner desire for more. That internal emptiness can only be filled when we are daily choosing to trust God to lead our life.

Choose the Right Path is a friend's website found at www.choosetherightpath.com. It's an interactive site where you can select *If you are still searching for answers...* OR *If you are ready for eternity...* If you're not a solid 100, then let's look at the "If you are still searching for answers" click.

He graciously gave me permission to share the information from his website here in this book.

Take the Good Person Test:

Do you think You're a Good Person?

Have you ever told a lie? Even for a good purpose?

What does that make you? If someone lied to you, what would you call them?

That makes you a liar. We might not like that word – we like to say we're "just human," or that we've stretched the truth." But the *truth* is – if we've told a lie, we're a liar.

Have you ever taken anything that did not belong to you? Even something small? Are you sure? A pen or pencil?

That makes you a thief. It sounds harsh, but the truth is – if we've ever stolen anything, we're a thief.

Have you ever looked at another person with lust or desire?

Jesus said, that makes you an adulterer. Jesus said in Matthew 5 that to look at someone with lust is to have committed adultery with them.

Have you been angry with another person? Jesus said that makes you a murderer. Jesus said in Matthew 5 that whoever is angry with his brother without cause is guilty of murder.

You might be wanting to push back or argue, but hang in there and let's keep talking this through. This is actually going to turn out with great news!

Have you ever taken God's name in vain? Have you ever used God's name as a curse word or to express disgust?

The Bible calls this blasphemy. According to God's standard, the Bible, that makes you a blasphemer.

You may not realize this... but those are just five of the Ten Commandments. By your admission and standard of God's law, the Ten Commandments, you are a lying, thieving, blasphemous, murderous, adulterer at heart. And you have to face God on judgement day!

If God were to judge you by His law, would you be innocent or guilty? Would you go to heaven or hell? The Bible says that all murderers, adulterers, thieves, and liars will have their place in the lake of fire – Revelation 21:8.

The Bible offers hope.
II Peter 3:9 says that God is "not willing that any should perish but that all should come to repentance."

Imagine you are standing in front of a judge, GUILTY of a serious crime. All the evidence has been presented and there is no doubt of your guilt. Your apologies and good works cannot erase your crimes; therefore, you must be punished. The fine for your crime is $250,000 and you have no money.

The judge is about to pass sentence when someone you don't even know rushes in and pays your fine for you! The court accepts the money and declares that you are free to go.

That is exactly what God did for you on the cross 2,000 years ago.

Romans 5:8 *"But God commandeth his love towards*

us, in that, while we were yet sinners, Christ died for us."

Jesus loved you so much that He paid the penalty for your sin so you wouldn't have to!

God has provided a way of escape, and that is through the gospel of Jesus Christ.

What must I do?

Repent of Your Sin
That means turning away from your sin and asking God to forgive you for breaking His law. Jesus said in Luke 13:3: *"Nay: but, except ye repent, ye shall all likewise perish."*

Refuse your own self-effort
Realize that there is no way you can work your way to heaven or somehow be "good enough" to earn heaven.

Ephesians 2:8-9, *"For by GRACE ye are saved through faith and that not of yourselves: it is the gift of God: NOT of words, lest any man should boast."*

Trust in Jesus Christ as Your ONLY Hope.

Trust in Jesus like you would trust a parachute if you were jumping out of an airplane. You wouldn't just believe in the parachute, you would put it on (trust it) and jump (act on it). That is how we must put our faith and trust in Jesus as our only hope of heaven.

Acts 4:12, *"Neither is there salvation in any other: for there is none other name under heaven given among men, whereby we must be saved."*

Receive Jesus Christ as Your Savior and Lord.

Turn your life over to him.

John 1:12, *"But as many as received Him, to them gave he power to become the sons of God, even to them that believe on His name."*

Today with all your heart, turn away from your sin, and surrender your life to Jesus Christ. Please don't put it off. You may die today and then it will be too late. Put your faith and trust in Him today.

II Corinthians 5:17, *"Therefore if any man be in Christ, he is a new creature: old things are passed away; behold, all things are become new."*

The former preschool teacher in me would like to summarize with the ABC's.

A – Admit you are a sinner

Romans 3:23, *"for all have sinned and fall short of the glory of God,"*

B – Believe Jesus is God's son, He died on the cross for you, and rose three days later from the grave

John 1:12, *"But to all who did receive him, who believed in his name, he gave the right to become children of God,"*

C- Confess Jesus is the Lord of your life. Commit yourself to following Jesus and serving others

Romans 10:9, *"because, if you confess with your mouth that Jesus is Lord and believe in your heart that God raised him from the dead, you will be saved."*

John 3:16-21 *"For God so loved the world, that he gave his only Son, that whoever believes in him should not perish but have eternal life. For God did not send his Son into the world to condemn the world, but in order that the world might be saved through him. Whoever believes in him is not condemned, but whoever does not believe is condemned already, because he has not believed in the name of the only Son of God. And this is the judgment: the light has come into the world, and people loved the darkness rather than the light because their works were evil. For everyone who does wicked things hates the light and does not come to the light, lest his works should be exposed. But whoever does what is true comes to the light, so that it may be clearly seen that his works have been carried out in God."*

For some of you, this may be more Bible verses than you have read in a long time or maybe ever in your lifetime. Where from here? Pray and open a Bible each day. Where to begin? Proverbs is a great place to begin, as there are 31 chapters which is (generally) one chapter each day.

Please do not close the book! Please allow me to finish sharing our unbelievable story, including the third house challenges. It's not all struggles, though, as there are some fun stories still to come!

13

CHOOSING TO TRUST AND BE THANKFUL

Seven houses since we were married. That was not our plan. There have been countless opportunities to choose to persevere and walk out our faith. Those opportunities continue to come daily in abundance. I think of an awkward conversation Craig and I were having about the house situation. It was towards the end of that conversation that our neighbor texted saying there was a full rainbow over our house. As I went outside to take a picture, there it was: vibrant colors with our house directly in the middle. It was a very timely reminder of God's faithfulness!

In our family, we often use the statement "What's the game plan today?" But we recognize that God is far bigger than a game plan for the day.

He has a God-sized plan, agenda, and big-picture vision for us. He is sovereign.

Let this sink in: God is more concerned about our heart than our happiness. In a recent weekly text encouragement, Tim Tebow said, "You never know what God is doing with your life, and you never know what He is preparing you for!"

He is God. We are not! He created the universe full of stars, moons, and planets. He created the deep oceans and the bodies of land and filled them all with living creatures. Yet, each one of us matters to Him. I don't know what God is up to, but I trust Him. He is the Creator of the universe, yet He can be personable and close to each of us daily. I choose to trust Him. When we choose to replace a negative thought with a positive thought, we are changing our reality.

Why would I take time to write out our story, with so many details I would rather forget? First reason: I want my sons and each of you to know that while life is unpredictable, we have a sovereign God who loves us, is faithful to us, and cares for us. Second reason: One particular day, I had a rare uninterrupted block of time to begin this book. The next day, I went with a friend to a ladies' night event at her church where a special guest speaker's message was to share our story for God's glory. My friend, who knew about the time I'd been afforded to write over thirty pages the previous day, chuckled as she leaned over and said, "Do you realize she's speaking to you?"

God has a story for you, too. He is always working even when we don't see it. Trust Him and live your life for His glory as He will never fail you or leave you.

> *"Trust in the Lord with all your heart and lean not on your own understanding; in all your ways submit to him, and he will make your paths straight."*
> Proverbs 3:5-6

> *"Many are the plans in a person's heart, but it is the Lord's purpose that prevails."* Proverbs 19:21

Guests were going to start arriving for my son's birthday party. It would be a NERF battle in the backyard. On this Saturday morning, January 25th, 2020, I was praying while applying my make-up and had just told God that I felt emotionally drained, as it had been a hard and trying week. Then, I looked down at my phone and saw a text letting me know of an opportunity to share about God's faithfulness in 2019 with our house and health journey. Wow! I was immediately reminded of a truth from scripture by my navy sign from Hobby Lobby: "In Everything Give Thanks" 1 Thess. 5:18.

I almost laughed out loud as I said to God, "Of course you want me to share while I feel drained and walking through the challenges of 2020!" So, I shared because I feel led not only to live out giving thanks, but to encourage anyone (including nudges to myself) who needs to be reminded of God's faithfulness – even (and perhaps especially) when things don't make sense.

Here's an excerpt from what I shared then:

> The home we built was done as Owner-Builder. This meant not only pulling permits with the county and meeting each inspector along the way, but also countless hours of sweat equity. There were insulation, window sills, tiling, installing interior doors and front door, fireplace stonework, shiplap and wood work, and custom benches, just to mention a few projects, along with what felt like 3,255 decisions that we made on everything from tile to door handles to wiring.

> Our to do list is slowly growing smaller, and currently our garage floor is covered in sawdust with more barn doors in progress. The home is beautiful and I so respect the hard work and determination

of my great husband. Our journey may appear flawless at first glance, with the blessing of a beautiful home, but 2019 was a really hard year for us.

It would make storybook sense to have this 7th house we've lived in be the concluding chapter of our house story where everything is easy, picture perfect, and all rosy. I am continuing to learn that God's plan is not typically what we expect.

Beyond the standard house projects, we have had our fair share of experiences that don't make sense. The week before we began hosting the middle school boys Bible study in July, our septic tank pump shorted out (contractors had plugged the wires in opposite of how they should be and fortunately had zip tied them together so there was no question that it was their mistake – which resulted in them replacing the septic tank). Four days later the well's constant pressure system stopped working.

Our driveway is lined with pavers. There was one paver that did not get concreted down (really?!). So, Craig called Concrete Hippie, the installer of the pavers. True to his brand, the man looks like a cross between a hippie and Santa Claus. Craig had had conversations with him almost every time he had come out to our house and they had usually ended with him telling Craig, "You pray for me."

Between the time we noticed the loose paver and Craig calling him to come out and take a look, I had a little God-nudge about our paver guy. I had been in my local Christian bookstore and Hippie came to mind when I saw an Experiencing God Day by Day Devotional on sale for two dollars. I bought it and wrote an encouraging note in the card to let him know we were praying for him and nudging him to take a few minutes out of his day for his very own talk with God.

A few months later, we were gathered in the church lobby when Hippie walked by. He shared with us that he had met a county inspector who offered to take him out to lunch. That thirty-minute lunch turned into two hours and he now comes to church every week. God is so good. I have praised Him many times for letting us see a glimpse of Him working in the details. Seeing Hippie even at a distance at church is a weekly reminder that God has used and is using our family to impact others.

So many times we don't get to see the details. Remember the septic tank power plug situation? Well, a few weeks after that, our neighbor noticed that there were two young girls messing with that same electric plug. They explained that they were trying to charge their cell phones, so he led them to our front porch to an unused plug, and there they told him quite the story of why they were on our property and were not wanted at home.

They left in an Uber right before we got back home, and we arrived right before the police officer showed up. While driving home, we were saying out of all of the houses in our area, why did they come to our house? Before the night ended, we learned that the story the girls had told our neighbor was made up, and that they were actually runaways from a few streets over so they were considered missing persons. Why? We don't know the whole story, but I do know that before the officer left our house, we stood in our driveway and prayed for the girls and their safety and for the officer. While we didn't know all the details, we were grateful to have been given an opportunity to stand in the gap.

As we meet with the air conditioning company this week and my garage floor is covered in sawdust, I know that this is NOT the story I would have chosen for our family. Many days, I have to pray away my frustration over the time and energy that our house journey has taken from us - from our family time and from our health. But I can't stay there with those thoughts.

Over the past year, I have had many opportunities to live out 2 Corinthians 10:5 and "Take every thought captive." I am far from mastering this principle and doubt I will ever perfect it here on this earth, but working at it sure does help me get through hard days.

When you visit our home, you will see in our front flower bed seven stones, each with a house number imprinted representing the seven houses we've called home. I need this visual reminder of God's faithfulness. Maybe you, too, need visual reminders around your house of scripture verses, pictures, or even memory stones. God is continuing to write your story, too.

You don't have to walk through my same circumstances to know pain, frustration, fear, discouragement, or hurt. Our circumstances are not an apples-to-apples comparison as you may have your world turned upside down by the loss of a loved one, car accident, job loss, frustrating ongoing situation, broken or hurtful relationship, or chronic illness in your child or yourself, just to name a few possible challenges.

I have struggled with 1 Thessalonians 5:18, "In everything give thanks" and humbly say that while I have not mastered it, I try my best to be intentional in my efforts. When the water pump on my van went out at 58,430 miles, my heart started flooding with thoughts of "Not again!" and "How can this be my second van in a row with a water pump going out at such low mileage?" Then, I stopped myself to take my thoughts captive and said, "Thank you, Lord, that this is happening before the warranty ends at 60,000 miles. I trust you."

We all have a journey. I challenge you, friends, to choose to be thankful – especially when it's hard. Choosing to be thankful is following a command in the Bible, so you will never go wrong with this choice.

14

THIRD HOUSE WAS A BATTLE

Life is not guaranteed to be smooth sailing. It definitely has not been for us. Our third house was a real challenge for us, with air conditioners not interlocked to allow fresh air in for a healthy level of carbon dioxide. The air conditioner challenge was always just one more thing on top of the other circumstances surrounding us during the first year and a half in our new house. The circumstances detailed in this chapter are not remotely a complete list, but more like a snapshot of our ongoing battle to keep up with our house challenges. This is all in addition to the privilege and responsibility of raising our three boys, the role of leading a private school, and being actively involved in both church and recreational sports.

First, there were the wildlife incidences:

*A fruit bat hanging from the air vent in the laundry room – and the mystery of how it got inside at all.

*A cricket chirping in the wall and moving throughout the house for two weeks day and night - but especially noisy at night.

*A black widow spider with three egg sacs on the back porch. Almost a year later, there was a second one in our garage and the next day, a third on our back porch. So thankful they were outside!

*A large bufo toad in our front yard, which thankfully we found before our dogs did.

* Our yellow Labrador retriever at the age of four had a growth appear on his lip and thankfully, after having to have it surgically removed, the vet's instinct was not correct and it was benign.

* The addition of a chocolate lab puppy after we were in this new house for several months. I could (and maybe will one day) write a whole series of children's books about this pup. His family line was bred for hunting; he successfully hunts and finds my toothbrushes and escapes through narrow places, and he did have a bad habit of "counter surfing", a trait we discovered when he ate my meat-loaf off of the kitchen counter when I walked into the garage.

*Fortunately, many of our animal visitors have been critters outside who keep their distance: a family of foxes, various gopher turtles, a family of sand cranes, and the owl hooting in the tree nearby at dusk.

Then there were broken big toes:

During the second month in the house, our youngest son broke his right big toe while running up the steps when he missed the first step. Two months later, he broke his left big toe when he dropped his hoverboard at the bottom of the steps. Needless to say, we had frequent practice in thankfulness – thankful that surgery was not needed and that he was a trooper with a walking boot – twice!

Lastly, there were the mechanical issues:

* Dishwasher leaked
* Refrigerator hose replaced twice
* Microwave sparking and serviced multiple times until they ended up refunding our money
* Bathroom leaked into the closet as the overflow was not sealed at installation – so thankful this was caught right away!
* Ceiling fan in bonus room stopped working and had to be replaced
* Kitchen sink leaked when the compost

bucket wedged by the pipe fitting – no more composting

* New dryer was serviced multiple times and they ended up refunding our money as they deemed it not repairable – not ideal since it had been purchased at a great price – maybe it was God keeping us from having one more gas appliance in the house when we didn't even realize yet that our house was exceptionally tight and the a/c ventilation had not been installed effectively

* Septic tank plugged into outlet incorrectly by installers, which shorted it out and they replaced it – so thankful they had zip-tied it, showing it was their mistake and not ours!

* Constant pressure system panel on our well stopped working from a manufacturer default

* Back porch tongue and groove detached and had to be fixed

* Downstairs a/c coils replaced

* Sauna heater (which was helpful for my mold detox protocol) stopped working after only a few months of use - thankfully it was under warranty.

* Refrigerator seal needed to be replaced as it had resulted in the temperature not staying cool enough at times for the meat (it's never good to realize at dinner time that your meat has gone

bad)

* Septic tank was backed up as the necessary filter clogged at the year mark. Typical maintenance is a cleaning every two to three years. The serviceman said the only other time he has seen it clog so early was a family who ate very healthy. We laughed and admitted that we were guilty of being such a family!

* Gas cooktop was leaking – replaced 3/5 of the fittings inside and when it was still leaking a few weeks later, then we requested a replacement as we couldn't trust it. The warranty company refunded it since it had been an ongoing issue and they were not able to get the replacement valves for an additional month or longer.

* iPhone 7 froze, resulting in pictures, notes and contacts being lost. The phone was STUCK with the apple on the screen! It is in a safe place in case I come across someone who can retrieve the pictures.

* The next month, my new phone had problems with the speaker such that phone calls were unclear for the person on the other end. Months after dealing with it, the store reopened after the spring 2020 lockdown and the phone was replaced.

* My husband's vehicle was at the dealership for

forty days with engine issues. When he received it back on day 40, the hood sensor dinged. It would ding while driving down the road. It would ding constantly when my son turned on his music with bass. I have fun memories of our family of five driving down the interstate, listening to music featuring the ding of the sensor. The faulty sensor was replaced, but it didn't stop the ding. This was our life until we decided to trade in the vehicle before the sixty-thousand-mile warranty ended. Unfortunately, his trade-in did not end vehicle issues for us. Within the next two months, he had a flat tire on the way to a job interview (nope - this doesn't just happen in the movies) and two weeks later, he was rear-ended.

I have had to intentionally remind myself that God was and is not surprised by any of these circumstances.

> **Whatever you are facing – your circumstances do NOT define you. The challenges we have faced certainly stole time from our family and energy from me, but I am counting on God to restore our time and my health, and to keep my family in His care. What are you facing?**

Our world bombards us! It teaches us to live in the here and now, and sometimes it sends messages that are not true, such as the idea that parents don't know anything, and the view that you aren't being mindful of others if you don't just hush and do what you are told. We have learned that we must listen very closely to all of the words and meanings we are hearing in our world around us.

Back in March of 2020, our President said that we were in an invisible war. The virus is not visible, but was he referring to more than the virus? I believe so. As believers, we know that the invisible war we fight is a very real war. It is spiritual warfare that has created fear and a host of struggles that can seriously interfere with gratefulness.

We know that Satan is on the prowl like a lion. The core of his strategy is lies, and they come in the form of deception, discouragement, doubt, and discontentment. The enemy wants to keep us deceived, discouraged, distracted, doubting, disconnected, disillusioned, and discontented in the dark areas of our lives. When we bring his lies into the light, they lose their power.

What do I mean by bringing deception from the dark to the light? It is recognizing it, communicating it to a loved one – maybe to our spouse or a trusted friend – and it's teaching our children to openly and frequently communicate. Another way to bring it into the light is to write it down. I call this a "brain dump." I typically sit at my computer and ramble my thoughts out – maybe even in disagreement. The result of this practice is that dark thoughts lose power when they are poured onto the page and not left in my mind. Once they are down, I can move on. This is one way I have practiced my scripture of the year as I strive to "take every thought captive." It is healthy and releasing. When we take our thoughts captive, it teaches our families (and us) to wire our brains to think about praising God and cultivating a grateful heart.

Circumstances. There have been many days when I felt like it was a DEMO DAY over and over. Like a bad movie playing on loop, I was constantly trying to tear down my hang-up on circumstances and instead focus on what was really important – my family and my health. Yet, the circumstances had to be dealt with – air conditioners, appliances, critters, (oh, my!) and more situations would not go away or resolve on their own. It's a life lesson in which I have had a lot of practice, yet have not mastered. I am persevering to get better at looking up at what really matters and not remaining in bondage to the to-do list and phone calls for resolutions on the pressing issues of the day.

Suffering and surrendering give us a greater

awareness that life is not about us and we are not in control. In this way, dependence upon God can actually be a beneficial result of our circumstances.

In the movie *War Room*, Ms. Claire serves Priscilla Shirer's character, Elizabeth lukewarm coffee. She explains that we like our coffee hot or cold – never lukewarm. Lukewarm for believers in Christ is only praying when they have a problem, twisting scripture to justify their sin, or viewing God like a genie in a lamp and what He can do for them. While they want to be a Christian because they are afraid of hell, they are not truly sorry for their sins. They frequently say not to judge, and yet they care more about what others think than what the Lord thinks. Revelations 3:15-16 (AMP) says, "I know your deeds, that you are neither cold (invigorating, refreshing) nor hot (healing, therapeutic); I wish that you were cold or hot. So because you are lukewarm (spiritually useless), and neither hot nor cold, I will vomit you out of My mouth [rejecting you with disgust]." There are far too many people who know the popular Bible stories and even attend church, but don't have a personal relationship with the Lord.

Think of people around you - maybe even yourself. Have they turned to the world for answers? How did that go for them? Are you drowning in

your circumstances with no hope? Give some thought to whether or not you are willing to follow James 4:8, which says, "Draw near to God and He will draw near to you. Cleanse your hands, you sinners, and purify your hearts, you double-minded."

As a family, we know that the world did not have any answers for our house situations, as even an insurance settlement did not give us resolution. A realtor could not find us a buyer and only until we fully surrendered and were down the final stretch of the journey did we have an offer - less than two weeks before the bank was to file foreclosure.

Satan wants to stir up strife and confusion. He wants to fill our minds and hearts with lies, hurts, and negativity. He wants to kill, steal, and destroy (John 10:10). The enemy's battle plan includes fear, idols, and sin, all of which open the door for him to gain a foothold. The enemy does not reign over our lives when we stand on God's Word, the Bible. We have to speak the Word of Truth aloud. We must fill our hearts and minds with God's promises.

God has won the battle.

Consider the words of Jennie Allen in *Get Out Of Your Head*: "But let me pull you in close and tell you that when you start taking risks for the kingdom of God and running your guts out, Satan will do everything in his power to discourage you. The devil delights in distracting us from worship, from running our races, because he knows that living out our purpose here is a direct result of our love for God, our whole-hearted focus on Him."

Again, this is not about being religious. This is about a relationship with God because I know that things in this world get corroded from gases, fall into sinkholes, get moldy, break down, don't make sense, and sometimes even have to be purged or demoed.

Most of us wouldn't entertain stealing, killing, adultery or any drastic offense. The enemy gets a foothold in way too many circumstances – through our thoughts, emotions, fear, worry, unforgiveness, deception, dishonesty (including "half-truths", because 80% truth plus 20% lie is 100% lie), gossip, adultery, gambling, pornography, lust, jealousy, pride, bitterness, and more.

Never forget that fears, unforgiveness, and negativity create an open door for the enemy.

What problem are you putting a band-aid on and avoiding dealing

with it? Don't be an ostrich in the sand with your head buried. It's not safe for you as a person. If you are a Christian trying to live your life to glorify God, then we need to bring the problem into the light and strive to be better used for God's glory. Don't let your thoughts, problems or others words define you!

Jeremiah 17:5-8 says *"This is what the Lord says: 'Cursed is the one who trusts in man, who draws strength from mere flesh and whose heart turns away from the Lord. That person will be like a bush in the wastelands; they will not see prosperity when it comes. They will dwell in the parched places of the desert, in a salt land where no one lives. But blessed is the one who trusts in the Lord, whose confidence is in him. They will be like a tree planted by the water that sends out its roots by the stream. It does not fear when heat comes; its leaves are always green. It has no worries in a year of drought and never fails to bear fruit.'"*

As we talked about with our boys, we are not robots. God gave us free will and allows us to make choices. God's word is our guide book. 2 Timothy 3:16-17 says, *"All scripture is God-breathed and is useful for teaching, rebuking, correcting and training in righteousness, so that the servant of God may be thoroughly equipped for every good work."*

Negativity, complaining, bitterness, and guilt do not empower God's mighty angels to fight our battle. Obedience and faith are keys to overcoming the struggles against the enemy. It was said to me by two different people on two different occasions, "Melissa, God has great plans for you and these enemy attacks are intended to debilitate you." This was confirmed for me while I attended the Proverbs 31 *She Speaks* online conference. Written in my notebook from the conference was: "God has been writing a story in your life for His glory" and "God is more worried about working something out in me than in the circumstances" as well as "stories transform, motivate and empower people." Then a quote from Meredith Brock, "Your weaknesses are not always your liability. They can be your doorway into intimacy with the people in your life. You just have to be brave enough to be vulnerable."

Sharing our stories and journeys leads to doing life with others. It breaks down the walls and masks of perfectionism, those notions that we all have it together or that certain others don't ever struggle with anything. Deceived, discouraged, distracted, doubting, disconnected, disillusioned, and discontented – these are the goals of Satan, and they only add to our struggles. Praying for spiritual eyes to see and spiritual ears to hear and then bringing those thoughts into the light breaks the power of that darkness.

"Think of it: Obedience to God without full surrender is an exercise in robotically following the rules. Surrendering to God without obedience is the equivalent of faith with zero works." – Jennie Allen, *Get Out Of Your Head*

1 Corinthians 15:58 encourages us: *"Therefore, my dear brothers and sisters, stand firm. Let nothing move you. Always give yourselves fully to the work of the Lord, because you know that your labor in the Lord is not in vain."*

Romans 12:2 often comes to mind as we have had numerous decisions to make along our journey. *"Do not conform to the pattern of this world, but be transformed by the renewing of your mind. Then you will be able to test and approve what God's will is—his good, pleasing and perfect will"*

Romans 8:18 gives us perspective of what is important in life: *"For I consider that the sufferings of this present time are not worthy to be compared with the glory which shall be revealed in us."*

A quote that really resonated with me is by Emily P. Freeman in *The Next Right Thing*: "I want to remember that true ministry is not something we do but is the overflow of an abiding life with God."

As we have walked through these very overwhelming

situations swirling around us, we have learned about the realness of spiritual warfare. The Bible tells us that Satan attempted to trick Jesus as he sought to be the most powerful. Satan's punishment was that he was cast from heaven. You might have heard him referred to as one of the fallen angels. Pride and his desire for power continually fuel an ongoing invisible battle between good and evil. Even though he is allowed to have reign on earth with the help of his demons, the great news is that we know the final outcome that he will be cast into the fiery pit of hell when Jesus comes again.

One of the most helpful resources for me to better understand this was Neil Anderson's book *Bondage Breaker* as it helped me learn how to pray more specifically. As Christians, we are encouraged by Psalm 91:11. *"For he will command his angels concerning you to guard you in all your ways."* Angels fight on our behalf when we are seeking to live righteously. God has been faithful and sovereign in my life. He will be in your life, too.

This prayer from Neil Anderson is a way to start each day, while allowing your own heartfelt words to be added in as you communicate and build your relationship with God.

> *Dear heavenly Father, I honor You as my sovereign Lord. I acknowledge that You are always present with me. You are the*

only all-powerful and only wise God. You are kind and loving in all Your ways. I love You and thank You that I am united with Christ and spiritually alive in Him. I choose not to love the world, and I crucify the flesh and all its' passions.

I thank you for the life that I now have in Christ, and I ask You to fill me with Your Holy Spirit that I may live my life free from sin. I declare my dependence upon You, and I take my stand against Satan and all his lying ways. I choose to believe the truth, and I refuse to be discouraged. You are the God of hope, and I am confident that You will meet my needs as I seek to live a responsible life through Christ who strengthens me.

I now take my stand against Satan and command him and all his evil spirits to depart from me. I put on the whole armor of God. I submit my body as a living sacrifice and renew my mind by the living Word of God in order that I may prove that the will of God is good, acceptable. and perfect. I ask these things in the precious name of my Lord and Savior, Jesus Christ. Amen.

Fixing my eyes on Jesus and taking every thought captive has been my daily goal through this ongoing battle. Hebrews 12:1-3 encourages us, "Let us throw off everything that hinders and the sin that so easily entangles. And let us run with perseverance the race marked out for us, fixing our eyes on Jesus, the pioneer and perfecter of faith. For the joy set before him he endured the cross, scorning its shame, and sat down at the right hand of the throne of God. Consider him who endured such opposition from sinners, so that you will not grow weary and lose heart." I was physically tired, but I did not grow so weary that I lost heart, faith, or perseverance. God is faithful and sovereign.

15

PRAYER MATTERS

Stillness and rest are words we don't often hear in our world. Stillness and rest allow for prayer and a time to recharge or prepare to face the day. Prayer is a conversation, and as with any other relationship, our relationship with God is strengthened by ongoing communication.

"Rest is trusting that God's got this, even if I'm a mess, even if I'm not enough, even if I mess up every day. Because I do." – Sarah Mackenzie, *Teaching from Rest*

"Margin is the space between our load and our limits. It is the amount allowed beyond that which is needed. It is something held in reserve for contingencies or unanticipated situations. Margin is the gap between rest and exhaustion, the space between breathing freely and suffocating." – Richard Swenson

There are books upon books written about prayer, so I will keep it simple as I share what I have learned about prayer on my journey. If you are unsure about praying, then I just encourage you to start. Pray by talking to God. Ask Him to show you that He is real and that He cares.

Looking back over my journey, I have asked myself "Why don't I pray more – and specifically, more *often*?"

On a family trip to South Dakota, we prayed as a family before bed. My prayer was that we would see something extraordinary the next day. While walking through a quaint western town, we came to the end of the main street and there was a GIGANTIC SPUD truck! Extraordinary! It was passing through that town and there we were taking pictures with this enormous potato!

A couple of years later, we were visiting Olympic National Park in Washington and went on a whale watch. The bedtime prayer the night before was to see something really great, really close, and if we could even see Orcas that would be extra special. On this dreary, rainy day, we boarded the boat and quite early into the trip, we saw humpback whales were very close to the boat. Showing off was a juvenile whale who was breaching and having fun. The guide announced to everyone on the boat, "You all are so lucky as it is very unusual to see a whale this close and this playful." Thankfulness filled my heart as there was no doubt that God answered our prayer. Soon afterward, the boat captain shared that Orcas were spotted some distance out, but if everyone had the time, he would take us there. Yep, God provided Orca sightings, too! Why don't I pray like this more often?

He is a God who does exceedingly abundantly more than we can ever ask.

We had not gone away to celebrate our anniversary in far too long. Here's an excerpt from our August 2019 blog post with the fun details:

While we don't watch a lot of television, we have watched Chip & JoAnna Gaines HGTV show where they took on many fixer-uppers and made a house feel like a home. With our past experience of remediating our Chinese drywall/ sinkhole house, redoing a foreclosure house where we lived for six years, then recently building our current healthy home for our family, we had in our mind that it would be fun and rewarding to work together and let our kids join in. We have great respect for the Gaines family, as we share their values of integrity, hard work, perseverance, and faith.

We were long overdue for an anniversary getaway. With Southwest Points, a Companion Pass (earned from spending so much on the house last year), and hotel points, we decided to explore all things Magnolia in Waco, Texas. My plan was to not have a plan and to go celebrate and explore with Craig. After an early morning flight on our anniversary, we went to Magnolia Table for brunch. With perfect timing, we did not wait long and enjoyed the friendly atmosphere. I had prayed for something extraordinary as God directed our steps that day. It was unexpected when our waitress introduced us to Ms. Stevens, Joanna Gaines' mom. As we walked out of Magnolia Table, we agreed it had been quite fun!

Our exploring began as we headed to the Magnolia Market, the Silos, and the Seed & Supply, relaxing under the covered patio while enjoying a White Peach Lemonade and Strawberries 'n Cream cupcake. A short distance away, we visited the Harp Design Co. and Shop on Bosque.

After relaxing at the hotel, we decided that a light dinner would be a good thing so we headed to a deli for a salad. That's where we had our truly unexpected extraordinary! The Gaines family was there eating dinner. While not wanting to be 'one of those people' to interrupt their dinner, we waited to say hello. Joanna took the baby out before we went over to greet them, but as Chip was leaving with the other kiddos, we said hello. A brief but friendly interaction confirmed that he appears to be the same on and off TV in his white t-shirt, jeans, and cowboy boots. He was even happy to oblige us with a picture!

Craig kept saying he couldn't believe the odds. I just wanted to know whose idea (Chip or Jo) it was to eat there as I knew it was an answer to my prayer for an extraordinary experience.

To me, this wasn't about a star-struck moment, but about a great opportunity to tell him "thank you for being a part of our faith journey." With our house journey over the past ten years involving a Chinese drywall/sinkhole house, redoing a foreclosure house and calling it home for six years, and then building our own modern farmhouse, it was after many hours of watching Fixer Upper that made it look fun and doable to us. As a family, we have listened to their books on audio, so our boys have heard their amazing story, as well as their hard work and never-give-up attitude.

So thankful for the time we had there on our anniversary with no crowd! So thankful for our no-stress getaway! So thankful for my husband who loves me, who is a great Daddy to our three boys, who has truly persevered through hard house situations, & who built - with tons of sweat equity and lessons along the way for our boys--a healthy home for our family!

You might say it's coincidences or happenstances, but I would have to suggest and believe that it was providence.

Fasting. Even though my husband and I grew up in church, we were not taught and did not have fasting modeled for us. This word is becoming more common as many health circles are using this word as you may hear intermittent fasting to refer to only eating a few hours during a day. Fasting as it is described in the Bible is very scriptural and powerful. This is not a theological definition. Personally, I understand fasting to be a committed effort to give up "something" as a reminder to pray and seek God's plan more. Food is a common "something" which may be one less meal a day, solid food for a designated number of days or a specific food or drink such as coffee. Coffee lovers starting their day in a different way begin their day with the reminder to trust God without their mocha latte or cappuccino boost.

The "something" does not have to be food-related but could be something you enjoy that perhaps pulls time away from you. A dear friend gave up Facebook for 21 days. When our boys were younger, we had a very freeing three weeks of no electronic usage, except for limited use for work. These examples are me just being real with what comes to my mind when I think of fasting.

I fasted when I was praying for resolution for our air conditioning issue - and for my marriage, too - because at this point, oversized house units and carbon dioxide levels had become a huge elephant in the room for us. It was a dreaded ongoing conversation. Fasting helped me to remember to diligently pray throughout the day.

Have you ever had to have a really

hard conversation with someone? The kind of conversation where your stomach is in knots? It was so hard to share what I had learned with my husband. He had worked so hard on this home for our family, had endured endless hours of mental and physical labor to make it happen. His own sweat-equity projects were all great - the issues were coming from the mistakes of the subcontractors. Regardless, we were both ready to move on with life and not deal with house issues after our past eleven-year journey. Those hard conversations are not easy. Words of encouragement and communicating that we are in this together are critically important. Words Matter!

16

YOU CAN HEAR GOD

God does speak. He's not audible like the person sitting next to you, but He speaks in many ways! God's words are the Bible. The Bible is made up of 66 books that were God-inspired and written by 40 men. It is a collection of stories that paint a picture. We learn from stories as they make an impression upon us. God speaks through His Word, circumstances, His Spirit, and people.

His Word: We have to open the Bible.

One summer day, I laid my Bible open to James 1. The next morning, I found it two pages over in Hebrews 12, which is subtitled *God Disciplines His Children.* I do not know the details of how my Bible was flipped two pages over, but I do know that we have to first open our Bible for God to speak to us through His

Word. Take it off of your nightstand. Dust it off from the bookshelf. Get it out of the car where you left it after church last Sunday. Open it and allow God to show, teach, and guide. Don't know where to begin? Read a Proverb each day? There's 31. As mentioned earlier, generally that's one for each day of the month.

Circumstances: I could list countless circumstances, but the first that comes to mind to share is that timing is not a coincidence. It was not coincidental that the offer on our Chinese drywall/sinkhole house came just over two days after our full surrender conversation and just a few days before the bank was going to foreclose.

It's not always a glaring "open door"; sometimes, it's many closed doors.

His Spirit: As a believer, the voice in your inner thoughts giving guidance is the Holy Spirit.

Priscilla Shirer shares in her book, _Discerning the Voice of God_, "He will give you the red light of conviction that means "stop"; the green light of ease and peace that means "go"; or the yellow light of doubt and uneasiness that means "wait." If you experience conviction in your life, celebrate! That means the Holy Spirit is there. He's working, guiding, and changing you! Even if His direction may sometimes be momentarily uncomfortable, He can see the entire picture of your life and will save you true disaster in the long run. He is steering you into God's will."

Liz Curtis Higgs says, "I know the Lord is speaking when I have a complete sense of peace, a sense of rightness at the very center of my being. Although I don't hear an audible voice, I feel a definite 'yes!' in my spirit. Not only will His unspoken words ring true spiritually and emotionally, but they will also stand in total agreement with His written words in the Bible. For confirmation that it's the Lord's voice and not my own fleshly desires leading me, I pray, search the scriptures, then share what I believe God has revealed to me with someone I trust. If their immediate response is, "Yes, absolutely!" then I can move forward with confidence."

People: Listen to people around you. The guy down the road whose life is in chaos is not the person to receive guidance from. The person who would give you input because of his/her own selfish gain is not the person to ask for guidance. Seek out the friend who you know is trying to live a life that honors God.

"When He begins to move, the results will be both immediate and obvious. You will know beyond a doubt that God is performing what He has spoken. And often the first change

137

you'll see won't be in your circumstances. It will
be in you." – Priscilla Shirer

Proverbs 15:31-32 says, "Whoever heeds life-giving correction will be at home among the wise. Those who disregard discipline despise themselves, but the one who heeds correction gains understanding."

In *Soul Detox* Craig Groeeschel explains, "Contrast toxic religion with the pure gospel. Religion is all about what I do. The gospel is all about what Jesus has done. Religion is about me. The gospel is about Jesus.

Religion highlights my efforts to do what is right. The gospel highlights what Christ has already done. Religion lures me to believe that if I obey God, he will love me. But the gospel shows me that because God loves me, I get to obey him. Religion puts the burden on us. We have to do what is right. A relationship with Christ puts the burden on him. And because of what he did for us, we get to do what is right. Instead of obligation, our right living is a response to his gift."

"Christianity is not a religion; it's not an ethical idea; it's not a psychological phenomenon. It's a person – Jesus Christ – who is in the business of changing lives." – Josh & Sean McDowell

You may know about Him, but do you know Him? I know beyond a shadow of a doubt that my journey is not one of religion, but one of relationship with my Creator and I will spend eternity praising Him in Heaven. Has your journey led you to know beyond a shadow of a doubt that you will be in heaven and not hell? He wants you to seek Him for discernment as you walk through each day.

Emily Freeman's simple yet profound statement rings true: "I'm convinced God is less interested in where we end up than he is in who we are becoming."

Making decisions is not easy. I have read this quote by Priscilla Shirer many times, which says, "If we truly believe that God will speak in the appropriate time, we should never feel hurried or pressured about making decisions that are not rooted in a deep-seated internal peace. If you are not clear, do not move. Only when God has spoken will you be cued to respond in obedience."

You can hear God. Prayer is communication with Him.

A missionary to India named Mary Geegh shared her 38-year experience and what God taught her about praying and listening as she shared in *God Guides*, printed by Pray America. One of my favorite stories she shared was when she prayed for how to help dissolve the tension she felt towards a colleague. She had the thought to "Take her a fresh egg." It was such a strange thought and Mary didn't want to offend her colleague. After she returned later in the day to her open-air house in India, a chicken sat nearby on a chair. It promptly cackled and laid a fresh egg. She remembered her early morning thought, but rationalized that her colleague would surely laugh at her. With a heavy tug on her heart to obey the thought, she took the egg and gave it to her son, who was playing outside.

Later in the evening, her colleague asked how she had known to send her an egg. Her own response was, "Oh! That's just like God! He knew I had nothing to eat today. There just wasn't enough food for all, so I went without. Then you brought the egg for me. When I ate it, I felt so satisfied and strengthened."

As a person who does not believe in luck or coincidences, I get so excited when God allows us to know how He is working in the details of our lives and those around us!

The prayer she shared isn't one to pray while you're driving down the road or in a hurry - which brings us back to being still and quiet. It's part of your prayer conversation with God, while you are sitting with no interruptions with a paper and pen in hand to write down what you feel God impresses upon your heart. Aloud, I read the scriptures listed below and then say the prayer.

God Guides Sample Prayer to Initiate Listening Prayer

Father, I come to you in the name of Jesus Christ, Your Son, and according to James 1:5 I am seeking wisdom for _____. In the name of Jesus, according to Matthew 28:18 and Luke 10:19&20 I take authority over Satan and his fallen angels and command that they be rendered deaf, dumb, and blind to my prayers and removed from my presence. I place my own voice under subjection to the shed blood of Jesus and command that my own thoughts be taken captive to the obedience of Christ, according to II Corinthians 10:5. I ask Father that only Your Holy Spirit will speak to me as I wait on you for wisdom, insight, and direction for ____ and what You show me and direct me to do, I will quickly obey.

James 1:5 – "If any of you lacks wisdom, he should ask God, who gives generously to all without finding fault, and it will be given to him."

Matthew 28:18 – *"Then, Jesus came to them and said, "All authority in Heaven and on earth has been given to Me."*

Luke 10:19&20 – *"I have given you authority to trample on snakes and scorpions and to overcome all the power of the enemy; nothing will harm you. However, do not rejoice that the spirits submit to you, but rejoice that your names are written in Heaven."*

II Corinthians 10:5 – *"We demolish arguments and every pretension that sets itself up against the knowledge of God, and we take captive every thought to make it obedient to Christ..."*

17

WORDS REALLY DO MATTER!

Words matter with other people, with myself, and with God.

From the semantics in the court case to the strangers I have met along the way – words matter. Thoughts within myself matter as they determine my beliefs, decisions, and steps I take. Words matter. My journey is not about me and it's for God's glory, so I need to remember that words truly matter.

One final story. The last day of that getaway to Blue Ridge ended with a memorable experience. Sleepily, I crawled out of bed with the blanket around me and went to the back porch where I could enjoy the quiet time alone. The mountains were still covered with clouds and the fresh morning dew settled like a blanket.

My attention was drawn to the abundance of spider webs between posts on the porch railing. 24 SPIDER WEBS! There was NO spider in sight! It made me think of two things. First, I didn't see the spider who created the beauty of the spider webs but I knew a spider had been there working overnight. Just like the spider, I don't see God but I see the splendor of His majesty and the detailed work He is doing in my life. Second, I thought of Charlotte's Web and how Charlotte's words in the web... SOME PIG, TERRIFIC, RADIANT, HUMBLE saved Wilbur's life.

WORDS MATTER!

RESOURCES

Bondage Breaker by Neil Anderson

Breaking Busy by Alli Worthington

Discerning the Voice of God by Priscilla Shirer

Get out of your head by Jennie Allen

Junior Discovers Integrity by Dave Ramsey

Soul Detox by Craig Groeschel

Teaching from Rest by Sarah Mackenzie

The Grumble Free Year by Tricia Goyer

Choosetherightpath.com

Goodpersontest.com

god-guides.com

GotQuestions.org

Made in the USA
Columbia, SC
30 January 2021

31953706R00089